one  heart

universal

wisdom

from the

world's

scriptures

one heart

edited by
BONNIE LOUISE KUCHLER

preface by SYLVIA BOORSTEIN
essays by ANDREW HARVEY

Marlowe & Company
New York

ONE HEART: *Universal Wisdom from the World's Scriptures*
Copyright © 2003 by Bonnie Louise Kuchler
Preface copyright © 2003 by Sylvia Boorstein
Introductions copyright © 2003 by Andrew Harvey

AVALON
publishing group incorporated

Published by
Marlowe & Company
An Imprint of Avalon Publishing Group Incorporated
245 W. 17th St.• 11th Floor
New York, NY 10011-5300

First published under the title *One Heart: Wisdom from the World's Scriptures*
by One Spirit in 2003. This edition published by arrangement in 2004.

Library of Congress Control Number: 2004109644

ISBN: 1-56924-403-0

9 8 7 6 5 4 3 2

Designed by Pauline Neuwirth, Neuwirth & Associates, Inc.
Printed in Canada
Distributed by Publishers Group West

For my mom,
whose insight taught me
that great treasures lie hidden
beneath the surface.

And for Phillip,
whose love is one of the greatest
treasures I've found.

contents

PREFACE   xi
EDITOR'S NOTE   xv
ACKNOWLEDGMENTS   xvii

1 from a heart of compassion . . .

INTRODUCTION   1
FEEL WHAT OTHER PEOPLE FEEL.   3
LOVE PEOPLE.   5
BE A FAITHFUL FRIEND.   8
HELP THE HELPLESS.   11
GIVE.   14
DO GOOD DEEDS.   17
DON'T HARM OTHERS.   20
SPIRITUAL PRACTICE: PRAYER BEADS   23

2 from a heart of acceptance . . .

INTRODUCTION   27
LOOK AT THE HEART, NOT THE FACE.   29
JUDGE YOURSELF, NOT OTHERS.   32

FORGIVE, AND LET GO OF RESENTMENTS.   35
BE IMPARTIAL.   38
OVERCOME HATE WITH LOVE.   41
LIVE IN HARMONY WITH EVERYONE.   44
BE TOLERANT OF OTHERS' BELIEFS.   46
Spiritual Practice: LOVINGKINDNESS MEDITATION   49

3   from a heart of humility . . .

INTRODUCTION   52
BE HUMBLE AND MODEST, NOT PROUD.   54
ADMIT WHEN YOU'RE WRONG, AND REPENT.   58
FIND HARMONY WITH YOUR SPOUSE.   61
HONOR YOUR PARENTS AND RESPECT YOUR ELDERS.   64
LOVE AND TAKE CARE OF YOUR FAMILY.   67
LEAD WITH VIRTUE AND CONCERN FOR OTHERS.   70
Spiritual Practice: HOME ALTAR   73

4   from a heart of integrity . . .

INTRODUCTION   76
EXAMINE YOUR MOTIVES.   78
PURIFY YOUR HEART.   81
BE HONEST.   84
BE TRUSTWORTHY.   87
DON'T STEAL.   90
DON'T COMMIT ADULTERY.   93
PRACTICE WHAT YOU PREACH.   96
DON'T BE A HYPOCRITE.   99
CULTIVATE A STRONG WORK ETHIC.   102
Spiritual Practice: SACRED READING   105

5 from a heart of faith . . .

INTRODUCTION 107

BELIEVE YOUR BODY IS TEMPORARY,
  YOUR SPIRIT IMMORTAL. 109

LIVE WITHOUT FEAR OF DEATH. 112

KNOW THAT TRUTH IS ETERNAL, UNCHANGING. 115

ACKNOWLEDGE AN ALL-KNOWING PRESENCE. 118

SEEK AND YOU WILL FIND. 121

RECOGNIZE A LOVING, UNIVERSAL PARENT. 124

COMMUNICATE THROUGH PRAYER OR WORSHIP. 127

ACCEPT THE EXISTENCE OF SPIRITUAL BEINGS. 130

Spiritual Practice: WORSHIP THROUGH SONG,
  DANCE, AND CHANT 132

6 from a heart of wisdom . . .

INTRODUCTION 134

KNOW THAT YOU ARE ACCOUNTABLE
  FOR YOUR ACTIONS. 136

ACCEPT THAT YOU REAP WHAT YOU SOW. 139

LEARN THE DIFFERENCE BETWEEN RIGHT AND WRONG. 141

AVOID WRONGDOING AND ITS CONSEQUENCES. 144

SEE YOUR LIFE AS A JOURNEY—CHOOSE A WISE PATH. 147

SEE YOUR HEART AS A GARDEN—PLANT IT WELL. 150

SEE GOODNESS AS A LIGHT—TURN IT ON. 153

CHOOSE YOUR COMPANIONS WISELY. 156

LEARN FROM A WISE MENTOR. 159

THINK FOR YOURSELF. 162

Spiritual Practice: LABYRINTH WALKING 165

7 from a heart of discipline . . .

INTRODUCTION 167

ACKNOWLEDGE YOUR INNER CONFLICT.   169
CONTROL YOUR THOUGHTS.   172
MEDITATE.   175
CONTROL YOUR WORDS.   178
BE AWARE OF THE POWER OF YOUR TONGUE.   181
CONTROL YOURSELF.   184
GUARD AGAINST LUST.   187
CONQUER VICES.   190
EXERCISE MODERATION.   193
PERSEVERE THROUGH ADVERSITY.   196
Spiritual Practice: FASTING   198

8   from a heart of surrender . . .

INTRODUCTION   201
ACCEPT CIRCUMSTANCES.   203
DON'T LET ANGER TAKE OVER.   206
GIVE UP NATURAL REACTIONS FOR
    SPIRITUAL BENEFITS.   209
BE CONTENT.   212
GIVE UP SELF-GRATIFICATION
    TO OBTAIN TRUE HAPPINESS.   215
DON'T BE GREEDY.   218
GIVE UP TRANSIENT RICHES TO GAIN
    EVERLASTING TREASURE.   221
DETACH FROM THE TEMPORAL;
    ATTACH TO THE ETERNAL.   224
Spiritual Practice: BREATHING   227

BIBLIOGRAPHY   231
PERMISSIONS   243

preface

i read *The Asian Journal of Thomas Merton* in the early 1970s, not long after it was published. I knew very little about Buddhism at the time, and being Jewish, my appreciation of Christian religious language only developed as an adult, but I still loved that book. I read and reread Merton's account of his meeting with Chatral Rimpoche, a Tibetan lama in Nepal, and it touched then—as it continues to now—what seems to me proof that across traditions, language, and culture barriers, through a translator who is not part of the conversation, it is possible to say, "This is the experience of my heart," and be understood by another person. Sometimes I think the limitations to Merton and Rimpoche's dialogue were an asset—they could not get lost in theology. I am comforted and reassured to know that human beings share similar wants and hopes. I think that interfaith dialogue would be so much simpler—and peace in the world so much simpler to achieve—if we could ask each other, "How do you feel when you say that? And, because you *feel* that way, what do you *know*, for sure?"

I've imagined, particularly in moments when I have known something with such certitude that I was sure I'd never forget it, that for others, similar moments have served as the building blocks of a given religious tradition. I assumed that spiritual lineages began with people feeling this same insight, thinking, "Now I Know!" and wanting to share their insights with the people they met. I assumed that insights were shared in local idiom, clothed in contemporary culture, and so the way truths are expressed and the way stories are told in separate lineages are particular to the time and place in which they began. Cosmologies and theologies, belief systems, are different. But what is fundamentally true about life and about human beings must be the same for everyone.

When I began practicing Mindfulness as a meditation, I wondered about how experiencing the insights that the Buddha taught—what my teachers said was the point of meditating—would be different from hearing or talking about them. "After all," I thought, "who doesn't know that everything is temporal, that giving is better than receiving, that morality is good for you, that acceptance and surrender and forgiveness are a relief?" And yet, in moments when I realized—directly and indisputably, "This is true!", I'd think two things. First, I'd think, "Experiencing really is different. Now I more than know. Now I (as my friend Reb Zalman Schachter-Shalomi would say) 'capital K' Know." And then I would think, "Everyone who pays attention will know this same thing."

I remember experiencing, in the middle of a Buddhist Mindfulness retreat, a feeling of profound awareness of the moment-to-moment arising and disappearance of phenomena.

"Aha!" I thought. "Transient are all conditioned things," which is the next-to-last sentence the Buddha said as a summation of his teachings before he died. I also remembered my grandfather's maxim, *"Gam Ze Ya'avor"* ("This, too, shall pass"), which I had long ago painted, in Hebrew, across a rafter of my kitchen ceiling, to support and encourage me when my four children were all very young. I have two religious vocabularies, and both of them rushed in to supply the words for my experience.

Words are a uniquely human way for information to pass from one person to another. My grandson Harrison is five years old, and if I say, in response to a question he has asked, "That's quite complicated," he will insist, "Explain it to me, then." Words cannot cause him to understand, but they can set up the conditions in his mind that allow understanding to happen. Buddhists would say, "The finger pointing to the moon is not the moon," but will go on to say that pointing helps direct the attention to the moon itself.

This lovely book is a collection of fingers pointing at this truth: there is a heartfelt peace available to human beings that expresses itself in a life of compassion, and there are universal instructions for its discovery. The Buddha's Sermon on Lovingkindness begins, "This is what should be done by those who are skilled in kindness and who know the path of peace." That everyone else's finger clearly points in the same direction is, especially in this very complex time in the history of the world, simply divine.

Sylvia Boorstein

editor's note

i grew up in church, which taught me spiritual values, and undoubtedly those values helped form me and shape my own beliefs. That was the good part. But the church also believed, dogmatically, that those who did not embrace its doctrine would ultimately be separated from God and everything good.

I couldn't accept that. It simply wasn't logical. Why would the same Creator who loves novelty—who saw to it that every sunset and snowflake would be unique, and that no human beings would ever think exactly alike—why would this creative Spirit demand that every person follow one rigid path?

It makes much more sense to me that, just as Spirit created natural laws that apply to everyone—such as gravity, motion, and aerodynamics—so there must exist spiritual concepts that transcend historical, cultural, and doctrinal boundaries. Guideposts, as it were, to help us along our own unique path.

Tracking through sacred texts as my hunting ground, I began searching for these posts, these core values we inherently share. The result of all that rummaging is now in your hands.

It's my hope that *One Heart* in no way trivializes the rich, genuine differences between religious traditions, or the importance of a belief system; yet this book should leave no doubt that these core values—values of the heart—are the common ground shared by all faiths.

My own belief is that in our diverse and often intolerant society, it has become important for us to identify these guideposts. What a grave negligence it would be to withhold core values from the education of our children simply because of doctrinal differences between adults.

My hope is that readers, upon seeing their own values vividly expressed by the sacred texts of traditions other than their own, will begin to understand the heart of Spirit, God, Allah, the Ultimate Reality, and take a step toward religious tolerance. If this book can plant the seeds of understanding into just a few minds—well, that's a few more blossoms of tolerance that'll sprout in this generation, each bearing the fruit of peace in the next.

Bonnie Louise Kuchler

acknowledgments

without the breath of Spirit, this book would not have been conceived.

Without the painstaking labor of translators all over the world, this book would not have been born.

Without the supportive, inspirational words of Sylvia Boorstein and Andrew Harvey, this book would not have blossomed.

Without the skilled, committed efforts of my agent, Tom Grady, this book would not have grown up and left home.

Without the vision and resources of Matthew Lore and Marlowe & Company, this book would not have made its way into your hands.

To each I offer warm and humble thanks.

note

quotes from the Old Testament encompass the traditions of both Christianity and Judaism. These will be marked throughout the book with the following symbol * .

one heart

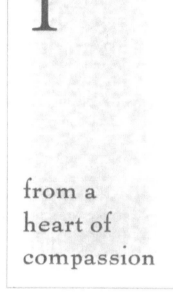

1

from a
heart of
compassion

all the religious and mystical schools of thought in the world agree with exalted unanimity on two linked things: that compassion is the sign and proof of real spiritual awakening, and that it is through the richness of compassion that an awakened being demonstrates his or her experience of divine love.

Perhaps the most profound story about compassion is the one that Jesus tells about the prodigal son who leaves home to fritter away his fortune in debauchery and ends up with less than nothing. When his father (who represents God in the story) sees his son return weary and forlorn, he doesn't merely forgive his son in a cool and detached way; his compassion for him is passionate, the outflowing of a tremendous love that nothing his son does—or does not do—can shake.

Through the wonderful details of that parable, Jesus shows us how unconditional God's compassion is and always will be, and he teaches us the kind of abandoned generosity with which we should act toward all.

When I think back on my life for examples of compassion, I remember one especially moving example. It occurred when I was a lost, miserable twenty-five-year-old traveling around South India. I found myself sitting on the steps of the Tanjore museum one morning with my face in my hands, waiting for it to open. There was a rail-thin old man in rags near me quietly sweeping the courtyard. I didn't pay any attention to him; I was too sunk in myself. When I did look up, however, I saw that he had placed beside me a cup of hot tea and two biscuits, a gift that must have cost him half his day's salary. He himself had disappeared, not even staying for my thanks. His act of pure compassion, which seemed to me that morning to rise out of a great knowledge of suffering, moved me profoundly, and I have never forgotten the joy and sense of being loved and honored that it brought me. I, who was so much richer in money than he, had hardly noticed the poor old man; he, who was so much richer than I in compassion, had not only noticed me but had seen that I needed help and sacrificed to give, without claiming any recognition for himself. His perfect act has perfumed my whole life.

Andrew Harvey

feel what other people feel.

LAY NOT ON ANY SOUL A LOAD

THAT YOU WOULD NOT WISH TO BE LAID UPON YOU,

AND DESIRE NOT FOR ANYONE THE THINGS

YOU WOULD NOT DESIRE FOR YOURSELF.

BAHA'I FAITH. *Gleanings, from the writings of Baha'u'lah*

CHRISTIANITY

In everything, do to others what you would have them do
to you, for this sums up the Law and the Prophets.

Matthew 7.12

ISLAM

Not one of you truly believes,
until you wish for others what you wish for yourself.

Forty Hadith of an-Nawawi 13

None of you have faith unless you love for others
what you love for yourself.

Hadith of Bukhari

BUDDHISM

Hurt not others in ways that you yourself would find hurtful.

Udana-Varga I.5.18

HINDUISM

You should not behave toward others in a way
    which is disagreeable to yourself.
This is the essence of morality.
All other activities are due to selfish desire.

Mahabharata, Anusasana Parva 113.8

JUDAISM

What is hateful to you, do not do to your neighbor.
This is the whole Torah; all the rest is commentary.

Talmud, Shabbath 31a

CONFUCIANISM

Tzu Kung asked: "Is there a single concept
that we can take as a guide for the actions of our whole life?"
Confucius said, "What about 'fairness'?
What you don't like done to yourself, don't do to others."

Analects 15.23

TAOISM

Regard your neighbor's gain as your own gain
    and your neighbor's loss as your own loss.

Treatise on Response & Retribution, verse 218

love people.

CHRISTIANITY

Everyone who loves has been born of God and knows God.
Whoever does not love does not know God,
    because God is love . . .
If we love one another, God lives in us
    and his love is made complete in us.

I John 4.7-8, 12

Clothe yourselves with compassion, kindness, humility,
    gentleness, and patience.
And over all these virtues put on love,
    which binds them all together in perfect unity.

Colossians 3.12, 14

ISLAM

Remember with gratitude Allah's favor on you,
    for you were enemies
    and He joined your hearts in love.

Qur'an 3.103

[5]

No one loves another for Allah's sake, without the Lord
who is great and glorious honoring that one.

Hadith of Ahmad

BUDDHISM

Just as a mother would protect her only child
at the risk of her own life,
even so, cultivate a boundless heart toward all beings.
Let your thoughts of boundless love
pervade the whole world.

Sutta Nipata 149-150

HINDUISM

Without love in the heart,
life is like a sapless tree in a barren desert.

Tirukkural 78

JUDAISM

Love your neighbor as yourself.

*Leviticus 19.18**

Be the disciples of Aaron—
one that loves peace, that loves mankind
and brings them nigh to the Law.

Abot 1.12

CONFUCIANISM

Compassion is the means by which you deal with everyone.
It is like a mother completely giving herself
   to the care of her baby.
She may not be perfect, but she won't be far off.

The Great Learning, chapter 9

Lack of compassion is very shortsighted.

Kongcongzi, chapter 4

TAOISM

Love the world as your own self;
   then you can truly care for all things.

Tao Te Ching 13

With a compassionate heart turn toward all creatures.

Treatise on Response & Retribution, part 1

⁓

be a faithful friend.

CHRISTIANITY

Some friends play at friendship,
    but a true friend sticks closer than one's nearest kin.

Proverbs 18.24*

No one has greater love than this,
    to lay down one's life for one's friends.

John 15.13

ISLAM

The believers, men and women,
    are protecting friends one of another;
they enjoin the right and forbid the wrong . . .

Qur'an 9.71

BUDDHISM

The one on whom you can rely,
    like a child sleeping on its mother's breast,
is truly a friend who cannot be parted from you by others.

Sutta Nipata 255

HINDUISM

The triple service of friendship
    is to take the friend out of the wrong path,
    to lead him into the right path,
    and to share in his misfortune.
True friendship is that which comes swiftly to the rescue
    in the hour of trouble,
even as the hand goes instinctively to hold the dress,
    when it chances to slip down in company.

Tirukkural 788-789

JUDAISM

A friend loves at all times.

*Proverbs 17.17**

Two are better than one . . .
    For if they fall, one will lift up the other.
Though one may be overpowered,
    two can defend themselves.
A cord of three strands is not quickly broken.

*Ecclesiastes 4.9-10, 12**

CONFUCIANISM

Three times daily I ask myself:
   "Have I been unfaithful in dealing with others?
   Have I been untrue to friends?"

Analects 1.4

TAOISM

Help your brothers and sisters, be faithful to your friends.

Hua Hu Ching 52

Be faithful, filial, friendly, and brotherly.

Treatise on Response & Retribution 172-175

help the helpless.

CHARITY—TO BE MOVED AT THE SIGHT OF THE THIRSTY,

THE HUNGRY, AND THE MISERABLE

AND TO OFFER THEM RELIEF OUT OF PITY—

IS THE SPRING OF VIRTUE.

JAINISM. *Kundakunda, Pancastikaya* 137

CHRISTIANITY

Religion that God our Father accepts as pure and faultless
    is this:
to look after orphans and widows in their distress
and to keep oneself from being polluted by the world.

James 1.27

When you give to the needy,
    do not announce it with trumpets . . .
do not let your left hand know
    what your right hand is doing.

Matthew 6.2-3

ISLAM

Give in alms of the wealth that you have lawfully earned . . .
not worthless things which you yourselves
        would reluctantly accept.

Qur'an 2.267

There is a man who gives a charity
        and he conceals it so much so
that his left hand does not know what his right hand spends.

Hadith of Bukhari

BUDDHISM

Enlightened beings are magnanimous givers,
bestowing whatever they have with calmness,
        without regret, without hoping for reward,
        without seeking honor,
        without coveting material benefits,
but only to rescue and safeguard all living beings.

Garland Sutra 21

HINDUISM

When help is given by weighing the recipient's need
        and not the donor's reward,
        its goodness is greater than the sea.

Tirukkural 103

Fortunate are those who save others
        from the devastating curse of hunger,
for they have thereby deposited their possessions
        in a well-guarded vault.

Tirukkural 226

JUDAISM

Do not be hardhearted or tightfisted
    toward your needy neighbor.
Give generously and do so without a grudging heart.
Be openhanded toward the poor and needy in your land.

Deuteronomy 15.7-11*

CONFUCIANISM

The noble-minded cultivate in themselves
    the ability to unload other people's burdens.

Analects 14.42

TAOISM

Relieve people in distress
    as speedily as you must release a fish
    from a dry rill [lest he die].
Deliver people from danger
    as quickly as you must free a sparrow
    from a tight noose.
Be compassionate to orphans and relieve widows.
Respect the old and help the poor.

Tract of the Quiet Way

~

give.

CHRISTIANITY

God loves a cheerful giver.

II Corinthians 9.7

Give and it will be given to you.
A good measure, pressed down, shaken together
   and running over will be poured into your lap.

Luke 6.38

ISLAM

Allah's Apostle was the most generous person,
even more generous than the strong, uncontrollable wind
   (in readiness and haste to do charitable deeds).

Hadith of Bukhari

Give gifts to one another, for gifts take away rancour.

Hadith of Tirmidhi

BUDDHISM

Even dust, given in childish innocence, is a good gift.
No gift that is given in good faith to a worthy recipient
    can be called small, its effect is so great.

Jatakamala 3.23

HINDUISM

Giving, simply because it is right to give,
    without thought of return,
at a proper time, in proper circumstances,
    is enlightened giving.

Bhagavad Gita 17.20

Those who deeply know duty do not neglect giving,
    even in their own unprosperous season.

Tirukkural 218

JUDAISM

One gives freely, yet gains even more;
    another withholds unduly, but comes to poverty.
A generous person will prosper;
The one who refreshes others will also be refreshed.

*Proverbs 11.24-25**

The righteous give generously without sparing.

*Proverbs 21.26**

CONFUCIANISM

The gift is in the giving. If the giving isn't equal to the gift,
    it's like no gift at all,
    for the gift isn't invested with your goodwill.

Mencius VI.B.5

TAOISM

It is the Way of Heaven to remove where there is excess
    and add where there is lack.
Who can take their surplus and give it to the people?
Only ones who possess the Tao.
Therefore the wise act without expectation,
    do not abide in their accomplishments,
    do not want to show their virtue.

Tao Te Ching 77

do good deeds.

IN GOOD DEEDS, PURE OF HEART, LIES REAL RELIGION.

SHINTO. *Genchi Kato*

CHRISTIANITY

What good is it, my brothers and sisters,
    if you claim to have faith but have no deeds?
Faith by itself, if it is not accompanied by action, is dead.

James 2.14, 17

Let your light shine before others,
    so that they may see your good works
    and give glory to your Father in heaven.

Matthew 5.16

ISLAM

Everyone has a goal to which they turn,
    so vie with one another in good works.

Qur'an 2.148

BUDDHISM

Good deeds will receive the doer
    who has gone from here to the next world,
as kinsmen receive a dear friend on his return.

Dhammapada 220

HINDUISM

The good deed that is done not in return,
    but in the first instance,
is more precious than anything in this world or beyond.
Nothing can repay that act.

Tirukkural 101-102

The touchstone which discloses one's greatness
    or smallness is simply this—one's deeds.

Tirukkural 505

JUDAISM

Repentance and good works are like a shield
    against calamity.

Abot 4.13

These are things whose fruits people enjoy in this world,
while the capital is laid up for them in the world to come:
honoring father and mother, deeds of lovingkindness,
    making peace between neighbors.

Jerusalem Talmud, Pe'ah 1.1

CONFUCIANISM

To be able to practice five things everywhere under heaven
    constitutes perfect virtue:
Gravity, generosity of soul, sincerity, earnestness,
    and kindness

Analects 17.6

TAOISM

The mind of the wise is free
    but tuned to people's need.

Tao Te Ching 49

The highest good is like water.
Water gives life to the ten thousand things
    and does not strive.

Tao Te Ching 8

don't harm others.

A PERSON WHO IS WITHOUT DESIRES AND DOES NO HARM

UNTO ANY LIVING BEINGS IN THE WHOLE WORLD,

IS CALLED BY ME "UNFETTERED."

JAINISM. *Akaranga Sutra 7.3.1*

CHRISTIANITY

Love does no harm to its neighbor.
Therefore love is the fulfillment of the law.

Romans 13.10

ISLAM

There should be neither harming nor reciprocating harm.

Forty Hadith of an-Nawawi 32

Hurt no one so that no one may hurt you.
Remember that you will indeed meet your Lord,
and that he will indeed reckon your deeds.

Hajj Khutba (Farewell Address of Prophet Mohammed)

BUDDHISM

All tremble at violence; life is dear to all.
Putting oneself in the place of another,
    one should not harm nor cause another to harm.

Dhammapada 130

HINDUISM

Abstention of injury—by act, thought, and word,
    in respect to all creatures—
compassion and charity constitute behavior
    that is worthy of praise.
The act or exertion by which others are not benefited . . .
    should never be done.

Mahabharata, Santiparva 124.65

Righteousness was declared for restraining creatures
    from injuring one another.
Therefore, that is righteousness
    which prevents injury to creatures.

Mahabharata, Santiparva 109.111

JUDAISM

You shall not murder.

Exodus 20.13*

When a man or woman wrongs another in any way,
    breaking faith with the Lord,
that person is guilty . . .

Numbers 5.6*

CONFUCIANISM

In following the Way,
　　the noble-minded treasure three things:
a manner free of violence and arrogance,
a countenance full of sincerity and trust,
a voice free of vulgarity and impropriety.

Analects 8.4

TAOISM

There are some people whose behavior is unrighteous . . .
with brutality they do harm and damage.

Treatise on Response & Retribution, part 3

In dealing with others, be gentle and kind.

Tao Te Ching 8

prayer beads

the word "bead" comes from the Anglo-Saxon word "bede," and it means "prayer." As early as 500 B.C., people began using beads on a string to count their prayers, and before that, piles of pebbles and knots on a cord. As we see in the chart on the next page, almost every major faith uses some form of counting device.

Prayer beads are made from seeds, nuts, berries, olive pits, bones, wood, wool, clay, plastic, glass, amber, ivory, semiprecious stones, and costly metals. They can be smooth, rough, round, oval, faceted, or irregular. Strands can range from 27 to 300 beads or knots. But although the number, arrangement, and materials of prayer beads differs with each religion, the concept of counting devotions is universal.

Whether we repeat a mantra, recite a rosary, chant the names of our personal diety or simply pray, a tool such as prayer beads provides a tactile motivation to complete our devotional goals. The pressure of the fingers on each successive bead keeps our attention from wandering, and the rhythm of the devotions leads us more readily into stillness.

We do need to remember that repeating a devotion a hundred times won't rouse Spirit to listen. Spirit listens when we pray with our hearts. The repetition is for our own sake; if we say "Grant me compassion" a hundred times, it helps us remember to be compassionate.

Spiritual Practice

TRADITION	NAME	BEADS
Hindu	Japamala ("muttering chaplet") or just Mala	32-108
Buddhism—Tibet	Mala ("garland") Trengwa ("to purr like a cat")	27-108
Muslim	Mesbah, Mesbaha, Subha or Tasbih ("To praise and exalt Allah")	33 or 99
Catholicism	Rosary ("rose garden")	50 or 150
Anglican	Rosary ("rose garden")	33 or 99
Orthodox		
• Eastern:	Chokti ("chaplet")	33, 50,
• Greek:	Komboloi ("group of knots")	100 or 300
• Russian:	Vertitza ("string")	103
Baha'i Faith	Subha ("to praise")	95

SPIRITUAL PRACTICE

SIGNIFICANCE	RECITATIONS
108 is the number of worldly desires to be overcome. Also used to count breaths.	Mantras, such as "Hare Ram, Hare Krishna" (Praise Ram, Praise Krishna) or Names of God.
108 is the number of worldly desires to be overcome.	Mantras, such as: "Om! mani padme hum"(Om! The Jewel is in the Lotus, hum)
Represents the 99 known names (attributes) of Allah; the 100th name is known only by camels (and they're not telling).	33 times each: "Subhana-llah" (Glory be to Allah), "Alhamdu-li-llah" (Praise be to Allah) "Allahu akhbar" (Allah is great). Or pray Allah's 99 names.
The full rosary of 150 beads was created to aid the monks in reciting the 150 Psalms.	The Apostles' Creed and six prayers such as "Hail Mary ..." and "Our Father ..." plus reflecting on the mysteries of salvation.
33 is the number of years Christ spent on the earth.	Prayers of your own choosing
A knotted prayer rope is used instead of beads.	"Lord Jesus Christ, Son of [the Living God,] have mercy on me, a sinner"
Modified from Islam's 99 beads.	Allah'u'Abhá" ("God is most glorious")

peace bede

here are fifteen timely prayers you could recite twice with a strand of thirty beads or a pile of pebbles, or a knotted string . . .

In the world, let there be peace.

May we overcome hate with love.

Protect those who must fight for freedom.

Grant courage to all who face hate.

Guide our leaders through difficult choices.

May we stand for what is right and fair.

Keep us from destroying ourselves.

Strengthen those who grieve.

Remember the hurting children.

May we offer tender words.

May our hands be quick to help.

Be our shelter in times of fear.

Heal our land; heal our world.

Grant us tolerance, wisdom, and compassion.

May we stand united upon this earth.

2

from a heart of acceptance

whenever I think of the virtue of acceptance, I think of my father, whose noble nature radiated the kind of dignity that needs no external support or exclusiveness. When he died, the unanimous testimony of the mourners at his funeral was that he had been one of "God's true gentlemen." People of all kinds and classes loved him because they knew he respected them and treated them with an unforced courtesy that was as spontaneous as his breathing.

Whenever I am tempted to judge or grow angry and dismissive, I remember a conversation with my father on a train in India, where we lived at the time. We were traveling, just the two of us, to visit the ancient caves of Ajanta and Ellora; I was enormously excited to have him to myself, since he was often away and worked very hard. My father took the opportunity, as we ate curried chicken sandwiches and mangoes, to instruct me on what he believed to be the real value of life.

"What I want you to be always, my son, is a gentleman," he said.

"What is a gentleman, Daddy?"

"There are four main signs of a gentleman, I think. Firstly, a gentleman is always courteous and respectful toward anyone, whoever they are and whatever their class or circumstances, because a gentleman knows that life changes and that tomorrow he may need someone's help.

"Secondly, a gentleman never criticizes anyone else's religion. Nearly all the violence in the world springs from people criticizing or mocking each other's religion; this is madness, Andrew. There is enough God for everyone and all paths are a way to God.

"Thirdly, unless he has to, a gentleman never confronts others with their faults; he spends his time examining himself and trying to change himself, not presuming to judge others who may be laboring under difficulties he cannot know or even suspect."

"And what is the fourth sign, Daddy?"

"When people hurt him, a gentleman never returns hatred for hatred but strives to forgive and love his enemies, bearing always in his mind the example of our Lord Jesus."

Of the many wonderful things said about my father after his death, the one that most moved me came from a poor Indian gardener. He approached me one day with tears in his eyes and said, "You are lucky to be your father's. God loved him because he accepted everyone."

Andrew Harvey

look at the heart, not the face.

THE WORLD SEES THE MOUTH; GOD SEES THE STOMACH.
AFRICAN TRADITIONAL RELIGIONS. *Igala proverb*

CHRISTIANITY

Stop judging by mere appearances,
   and make a right judgment.

John 7.24

As for those who seemed to be important—
   whatever they were makes no difference to me;
God does not judge by external appearances.

Galatians 2.6

ISLAM

Allah does not look to your faces and your wealth
   but he looks to your heart and to your deeds.

Hadith of Muslim

BUDDHISM

Though people's faces and forms are handsome
    or beautiful, with words that flow easily,
do not consider them admirable if they are jealous,
    mean, and brutish.

Dhammapada 262

HINDUISM

The arrow is straight but cruel; the lute is crooked but sweet.
Therefore, judge people by their acts, not their appearance.

Tirukkural 279

What good is a body perfect in outer ways,
    if inwardly it is impaired by lack of love?

Tirukkural 79

JUDAISM

Do not consider appearance or height . . .
People look at the outward appearance,
    but the Lord looks at the heart.

I Samuel 16.7*

CONFUCIANISM

Inferior people try to disguise themselves,
    concealing their evil, and displaying what is good.
The noble-minded behold them,
    as if seeing their heart and reins.

The Great Learning, Commentary

When virtue excels, the outward form is forgotten.

Chuang Tzu 5

A dog is not reckoned good because it barks well;
    and people are not reckoned wise
    because they speak skillfully.

The Writings of Chuang Tzu, book XXIV.III.II.10

judge yourself, not others.

CHRISTIANITY

In the same way you judge others, you will be judged.
Why do you look at the speck of sawdust
    in your neighbor's eye
    and pay no attention to the plank in your own eye?
How can you say to your neighbor,
    "Let me take the speck out of your eye,"
    when all the time there is a plank in your own eye?

Matthew 7.2-4

ISLAM

Happy are the people who find fault with themselves
    instead of finding fault with others.

Hadith

You have been raised to deal with people gently
    and you have not been raised to deal with them harshly.

Hadith of Bukhari

BUDDHISM

It is easy to see the faults of others,
    but your own are difficult to see.
You carefully sift through others' faults
    but you hide your own like loaded dice.
When you focus on the faults of others,
    your perceptions soon become distorted,
    increasing your own imperfections.

Dhammapada 252-253

HINDUISM

If people would see their own faults
    as they see the faults of others,
truly, evil would come to an end in this world.

Tirukkural 190

The vile are ever prone to detect the faults of others,
    though they be as small as mustard seeds,
and persistently shut their eyes against their own,
    though they be as large as Vilva fruit.

Garuda Purana 112

JUDAISM

Do not judge your companion until you are in his place.

Abot 2.4

CONFUCIANISM

The disease of people is this: They neglect their own fields
    and go to weed the fields of others.
What they require from others is great,
    while what they lay upon themselves is light.

Mencius VII.B.32

TAOISM

Perfect integrity is not critical of others.

Chuang Tzu 2

Before you have strengthened your own character,
    what leisure have you to attend to the doings
    of wicked people?

Chuang Tzu 4

forgive, and let go of resentments.

THOSE WHO DO NOT ABANDON MERCY

WILL NOT BE ABANDONED BY ME.

SHINTO. *Oracle of the Kami of Itsukushima*

CHRISTIANITY

Forgive your brother and sister from your heart.

Matthew 18.35

Peter came to Jesus and asked, "Lord, how many times
    should I forgive my brother or sister when they sin
    against me? Up to seven times?"
Jesus answered, "I tell you, not seven times,
    but seventy times seven."

Matthew 18.21-22

ISLAM

If a person forgives and makes reconciliation,
    a reward is due from Allah.

Qur'an 42.40

The best deed of a great person is to forgive and forget.

Shiite. *Nahjul Balagha, saying 201*

BUDDHISM

Resentment cannot be removed by more resentment;
  resentment can be removed only by forgetting.

Mahavagga 10

Those who with forgiveness bear up
  under reproach, abuse, and punishment,
and who look upon patience as their army,
  and strength as their force—
those I call Brahmins.

Dhammapada 399

HINDUISM

Forgive transgressions always;
  better still, forget them.

Tirukkural 152

JUDAISM

For whom does God pardon iniquity?
For the one who pardons transgression in others.

Rosh Hashanah 17.A

He who takes vengeance or bears a grudge
  acts like someone who,
having cut one hand while handling a knife,
  avenges himself by stabbing the other hand.

Jerusalem Talmud, Nedarim 9.4

CONFUCIANISM

If you expect great things of yourself
    and demand little of others,
you'll keep resentment far away.

Analects 15.15

TAOISM

When conflict is reconciled, some hatred remains;
How can this be put right?
The wise accept less than is due
    And do not blame or punish;
For love seeks agreement
    Where justice seeks payment.

Tao Te Ching 79

be impartial.

GOD'S RAIN FALLS EVEN ON THE WITCH.

AFRICAN TRADITIONAL RELIGIONS. *Tanzanian proverb*

CHRISTIANITY

Be children of your Father in heaven,
    for he makes his sun rise on the evil and on the good,
    and sends rain on the righteous and on the unrighteous.
For if you love those who love you,
    what reward will you get?
Are not even the tax collectors doing that?

Matthew 5.45

ISLAM

The earth which bears you
    and the sky which overshadows you
    are obedient to their sustainer (Allah).
They have not been bestowing their blessings on you
    for any feeling of pity on you
    or any inclination toward you,
    nor for any good which they expect from you.

Shiite. Nahjul Balagha, sermon 142

BUDDHISM

That great cloud rains down on all
  whether their nature is superior or inferior.
The light of the sun and the moon
  illuminates the whole world,
both those who do well and those who do ill,
both those who stand high and those who stand low.

Lotus Sutra, chapter 5

HINDUISM

What good did the creatures of the earth do to the clouds
  that pour the rain?
So indeed should you serve society, seeking no return.

Tirukkural 211

The Earth supports all created beings equally.

Laws of Manu 9.311

JUDAISM

Rain is for both the righteous and the wicked.

Taanith 7a

Is God not the One who shows no partiality to princes
  and does not favor the rich over the poor,
for they are all the work of his hands?

Job 34.18-19*

When rain falls on our public land,
    it also falls on our private land.

Mencius III.A.3

Heaven and earth join,
    and gentle rain falls,
beyond the command of anyone,
    evenly upon all.

Tao Te Ching 32

overcome hate with love.

IF THERE IS CAUSE TO HATE SOMEONE,

THE CAUSE TO LOVE HAS JUST BEGUN.

AFRICAN TRADITIONAL RELIGIONS.

Wolof proverb (Senegal)

CHRISTIANITY

Love your enemies, do good to those who hate you,
   bless those who curse you,
   pray for those who mistreat you.

Luke 6.27-28

Do not be overcome by evil, but overcome evil with good.

Romans 12.21

A gentle answer turns away wrath.

Proverbs 15.1*

ISLAM

Requite evil with good,
   and the one who is your enemy will become
   your dearest friend.

Qur'an 41.34

BUDDHISM

Hate is not conquered by hate: hate is conquered by love.
This is a law eternal.

Dhammapada 5

HINDUISM

Does not the earth support the person that is engaged in
    digging it?
It is proper that we too bear with those who wrong us.

Tirukkural 151

Of what gain is perfect goodness
    if it does not do good to all,
        even to those who have done painful things to others?

Tirukkural 987

JUDAISM

God said, "Resemble me; just as I repay good for evil
    so do you also repay good for evil."

Exodus, Rabbah 26.2

If your enemies are hungry, give them food to eat;
    if they are thirsty, give them water to drink.

*Proverbs 25.21**

Hatred stirs up strife, but love covers all offenses.

*Proverbs 10.12**

Humanity overcomes inhumanity
　　the way water overcomes fire.

Mencius VI.A.18

Return love for hate.

Tao Te Ching 63

The wise are good to people who are good.
They are also good to people who are not good.
This is the power of goodness.

Tao Te Ching 49

live in harmony with everyone.

IT IS NO LONGER GOOD ENOUGH TO CRY PEACE,

WE MUST ACT PEACE, LIVE PEACE, AND LIVE IN PEACE.

NATIVE AMERICAN RELIGIONS. *Shenandoah proverb*

CHRISTIANITY

If it is possible, as far as it depends on you,
    live at peace with everyone.

Romans 12.18

Let us make every effort to do what leads to peace.

Romans 14.19

ISLAM

Hold fast, all together,
    by the rope which Allah stretches out for you,
and do not be divided among yourselves . . .
Let there spring from you a community
    inviting to all that is good,
        enjoining what is right, and forbidding what is wrong.
Such people will surely triumph.

Qur'an 3.103-104

BUDDHISM

Happy is the life of those who live in harmony.

Dhammapada 194

HINDUISM

Let your aims be common,
    and your hearts of one accord,
and all of you be of one mind,
    so you may live well together.

Rig Veda 10.191.4

JUDAISM

How good and pleasant it is
    when kindred live together in unity!
. . . For there the Lord bestows his blessing,
    even life forevermore.

Psalm 133.1, 3*

"Seek peace and pursue it" (Ps. 34.14).
Not only do you seek peace for your own locale,
    but you must pursue it in another.

Leviticus Rabbah IX.IX

CONFUCIANISM

My doctrine is that of an all-pervading unity.

Analects 4.15

TAOISM

Who regards self as the world may accept the world.

Tao Te Ching 13

[45]

be tolerant of others' beliefs.

CHRISTIANITY

God shows no partiality, but in every nation
anyone who fears him and does what is right
is acceptable to him.

Acts 10.34-35

Everyone who does what is right is righteous.

I John 3.7

The only thing that counts is faith expressing itself
through love.

Galatians 5.6

ISLAM

Allah is our Lord and your Lord. We have our own works
and you have yours;
let there be no argument between us.
Allah will bring us all together,
for unto our Lord is the journeying.

Qur'an 42.15

Would you dispute with us about Allah,
   who is our Lord and your Lord?
We will both be judged by our works.

Qur'an 2.139

BUDDHISM

One should never engage in frivolous debate
   over the various doctrines
   or dispute or wrangle over them.
With regard to all living beings
   one should think of them with great compassion.

The Lotus Sutra, chapter 14

To be attached to a certain view
   and to look down upon others' views as inferior—
this the wise call a fetter.

Sutta Nipata 798

HINDUISM

In whatever way people approach me,
   in that way do I assist them;
but whatever the path taken by people,
   that path is mine.

Bhagavad Gita 4.11

Like the bee, gathering honey from different flowers,
   the wise accept the essence of different scriptures
   and see only the good in all religions.

Bhagavata Purana 11.3

JUDAISM

One who is pleasing unto other people is pleasing unto God.

Abot 3.3

Anyone in whom are these three traits
    is one of the disciples of Abraham, our father . . .
(1) a generous spirit, (2) a modest mien,
    and (3) a humble soul.
[The disciples of Abraham] inherit the world to come.

Abot 5.19

CONFUCIANISM

The noble-minded are all-encompassing,
    not stuck in doctrines . . .
The noble-minded are principled, but never dogmatic.

Analects 2.14, 15.37

The problem with clinging to a single doctrine
    is that it plunders the Way.

Mencius VII.A.26

TAOISM

If you know the eternal law, you are tolerant;
being tolerant, you are impartial;
being impartial, you are kingly;
being kingly, you are in accord with nature;
being in accord with nature, you are in accord with Tao;
being in accord with Tao, you are eternal.

Tao Te Ching 16

lovingkindness meditation

meditation practices of Eastern traditions often require that we focus our mind on nothing, while Western religions tell us to focus on something. Either way, meditation gives us the focus to reign in our feral minds.

Through meditation—East or West—we purge negative thoughts, either by displacing them with healthy thoughts or by connecting with a consciousness above the plane on which negative thoughts thrive.

The Psalmist sang, *"we meditate on your unfailing love."* In Judaism, when we plant the seed of *Hitbonenut* (meditation), we reap two kinds of fruit: a release from ego, self-centeredness, and self-debasement, which interfere with our ability to love; and a new heart full of love for all of Spirit's creation.

Taoist meditation stresses *jing*, or quiet, stillness and calm; and *ding*, which is concentration and focus. This practice rewards us with spiritual awareness of the ultimate nature of the mind—open, clear, infinite, and unimpeded.

A Hindu meditator experiences insight into the unity of Reality—a realization that Spirit resides in all of creation. This powerful insight translates into love and service toward all beings.

Buddhism teaches that emotions are habits; they are actively created. Sometimes our language makes us think that emotions arrive unbidden: We are "overcome" with anger. We "fall" in love. We feel "depressed." Who do we think is doing the "depressing"? When we think about who and what we hate, we feel angry and self-righteous. We didn't just "fall" into anger; we cultivated it. The good news is, we can produce positive, loving emotions as well.

Buddhists practice *Metta Bhavana*, a meditation that helps us to empathize, forgive, and appreciate. Knowing that hatred cannot coexist with lovingkindness, we learn to concentrate on positive qualities rather than faults. Ultimately we cultivate loving, accepting feelings equally toward all people. Another term for this practice is "Lovingkindness Meditation."

MEDITATION

1. Sit cross-legged on the floor with your back straight. If you prefer to use a chair, make sure your feet rest flat on the floor, and don't lean against the back of the chair. Place your hands in your lap.

2. Relax from head to toe, or from toe to head.

3. Resolve to ignore all distractions, external and internal.

4. Project thoughts of lovingkindness. There are several ways to arouse these feelings toward others and yourself. Try any or all of these:

   ◆ Visualization. Conjure up a mental image of the person smiling.
   ◆ Reflection. Think about the person's positive qualities and any acts of kindness they have done.

- ◆ Affirmation. Repeat words like these for about five minutes:

    May _____(insert name) be filled with
    lovingkindness.

    May _____(insert name) be safe.

    May _____(insert name) be peaceful and happy.

    May _____(insert name) be healthy and strong.

5. You can project lovingkindness in many directions:

    - ◆ to yourself
    - ◆ to a friend or person you respect
    - ◆ to an indifferent acquaintance
    - ◆ to a hostile or unpleasant person
    - ◆ to a group of people—a particular race, religion, or
      age group
    - ◆ to all people.

6. Start with yourself. This is not a selfish thing to do! You
   need to develop a loving acceptance of yourself, before you
   can accept others unconditionally. Then continue by send-
   ing lovingkindness to other people in the order above, from
   easiest to hardest. This process breaks down the mental barriers we erect between different types of people and helps us
   love and accept all people equally.

3

from a heart of humility

at a time when many teachers in all the traditions parade their so-called "realization" and enlightenment with arrogance, and when the prevailing world-culture stresses self-assertion, power, and celebrity as the real virtues, it is hard to remember that humility is, as the great Persian poet Rumi said, "The only door into the room of divine life."

In a conversation with his disciples, Rumi once remarked that human and divine life were to be found in two adjoining rooms separated only by a thin wall. "There is a door through to the next room, the room of God—for everyone—and it is in the shape you make when you are walking on your knees toward God. Learning how to walk on your knees is the essence of the religious life."

Rumi has been my heart-friend and teacher for nearly thirty years. What has come to move me most is not his stupendous poetry, or the brilliance of his mind, or the greatness of his mystical powers. I am awed by them, of course, but what keeps breaking my heart open to him and makes me want to keep him at the core of my life is a quality that irradiates story after story about him—his great and real humility.

There is a story about Rumi that perfectly captures this virtue. A young man had heard of Rumi's mystical power and walked from Constantinople to Konya (about three hundred miles) to meet him. Coming into Konya, he saw an old man walking toward him whom he immediately recognized as the Great One. Immediately he prostrated himself before Rumi in the dust. When he got up, he saw that Rumi too, had prostrated himself before him. This went on thirty-two times until the young man cried out, "What on Earth are you doing? I am no one and you are the king of Mystics. How can you prostrate yourself before me?"

Rumi answered, "Why shouldn't I prostrate myself before a servant of my Beloved? Didn't the Prophet say, 'Blessed is he who is chaste in his beauty and humble in his honor'"? Then, Rumi added softly, "And if I had not shown you my nothingness, what would I be useful for?"

Andrew Harvey

be humble and modest, not proud.

HUMILITY IS MY MACE;

TO BECOME THE DUST UNDER EVERYONE'S FEET IS MY DAGGER.

THESE WEAPONS NO EVILDOER DARE WITHSTAND.

SIKHISM. *Guru Granth Sahib, Sorath, p. 628*

CHRISTIANITY

Do nothing from selfish ambition or conceit,
but in humility regard others as better than yourselves.

Philippians 2.3

Clothe yourselves with humility toward one another . . .
Humble yourselves, therefore, under God's mighty hand
that he may lift you up in due time.

I Peter 5.5-6

ISLAM

Do not walk proudly on the earth.

Qur'an 17.37

Let your gait be modest and your voice low:
The most hideous of voices is the braying of the ass.

Qur'an 31.19

If you have in your heart as much pride
    as a grain of mustard seed,
you will not enter paradise.

Hadith of Muslim

Give up anger; renounce pride;
    transcend all worldly attachments.

Dhammapada 221

There are two inner methods that can save all
    who practice them—
one is humility and the other is shame.
Those who have a sense of shame will do no evil,
    while those who have a sense of humility
    will never lead others to evil.

Mahaparinirvana Sutra

Humility and pleasant words are the jewels that
    adorn a person; there are none other.

Tirukkural 95

Shun all pride and jealousy.

Bhagavata Purana 11.4

Be humble, be harmless . . .
    aware of the weakness in mortal nature.

Bhagavad Gita 13.7-8

JUDAISM

Be of an exceedingly humble spirit,
    for the end of a person is the worm.

Abot 4.4

Pride goes before destruction,
    and a haughty spirit before a fall.

Proverbs 16.18*

What does the Lord require of you?
To act justly and to love mercy and to walk humbly
    with your God.

Micah 6.8*

CONFUCIANISM

The sense of humility and deference is the starting point
    of propriety.

Mencius II.A.6

The humane are high-minded, not proud:
    the vulgar are proud, but not high-minded.

Analects 13.26

TAOISM

Those who try to outshine others dim their own light . . .
Those who boast of their accomplishments diminish the
    things they have done.

Tao Te Ching 24

How can one liberate the many?
    By first liberating one's own being.
You do this not by elevating yourself,
    but by lowering yourself . . .
you become a master of simplicity, modesty, truth.

Hua Hu Ching 77

⁓

admit when you're wrong, and repent.

PEOPLE SHOULD KEEP IN REMEMBRANCE

THE ACCOMPLISHMENT OF REPENTANCE.

EVERY TIME THAT A SIN LEAPS FROM CONTROL

IT IS NECESSARY TO ACT . . .

ZOROASTRIANISM. *Sad Dar 45.1*

CHRISTIANITY

Godly grief produces a repentance that leads to salvation
and brings no regret.

II Corinthians 7.10

Produce fruit in keeping with repentance.

Luke 3.8

ISLAM

Whosoever repents and does good,
    truly repents toward Allah with true repentance.

Qur'an 25.71

Allah loves those who turn to him in repentance.

Qur'an 2.222

BUDDHISM

If one hides the evil, it adds and grows.
If one bares it and repents, the sin dies out.

Mahaparinirvana Sutra 560

He whose evil deeds are covered by good deeds,
    brightens up this world,
    like the moon when freed from clouds.

Dhammapada 173

If you wish to untie a knot,
    you must first understand how it was tied.

Surangama Sutra

HINDUISM

Whoever has committed a sin and has repented,
    is freed from that sin,
but you are purified only by ceasing, and thinking
    "I will do so no more."

Laws of Manu 11.231

JUDAISM

The concrete realization of wisdom
    lies in repentance and good deeds.

Berakhot 17

If my people who are called by my name
    humble themselves, and pray and seek my face,
    and turn from their wicked ways,
then I will hear from heaven,
    and will forgive their sin and heal their land.

2 Chronicles 7.14*

CONFUCIANISM

When the noble-minded make a mistake,
    they don't hesitate to correct it.

Analects 1.8

TAOISM

If you repent and start on a righteous march onward,
    you will certainly become a just person.

Treatise on Response & Retribution, Moral Tales 6

Those who have done evil deeds
    should now mend and repent.
If evil be no longer practiced and good deeds done,
    and if in this way they continue and continue,
they will surely obtain happiness.

Treatise on Response & Retribution 7

Find harmony with your spouse.

THEY ALONE ARE CALLED HUSBAND AND WIFE,

WHO HAVE ONE LIGHT IN TWO BODIES.

SIKHISM. *Guru Granth Sahib, Suhi Chhant, p. 788*

CHRISTIANITY

If a house is divided against itself, that house cannot stand.

Mark 3.25

Each of you should love his wife as himself,
   and a wife should respect her husband.

Ephesians 5.33

Let marriage be held in honor by all.

Hebrews 13.4

ISLAM

Allah created mates for you from yourselves
   that you might find quiet of mind in them,
   and he put between you love and compassion.

Qur'an 30.21

The best of you are the kindest of you to their spouses.

Hadith of Tirmidhi

BUDDHISM

When both are faithful and generous, self-restrained,
  of righteous living,
they come together as husband and wife,
  full of love for each other.
Many blessings come their way;
  they dwell together in happiness.

Anguttara Nikaya 55

HINDUISM

Place me within your heart;
  may one mind be in common to us both!

Atharva Veda 4.7.36

Be not parted—growing old, taking thought,
  thriving together, moving under a common yoke,
come speaking sweetly to one another;
I'll make you have one aim and be of one mind.

Atharva Veda 3.30

JUDAISM

A man will leave his father and mother
  and be united to his wife,
and they will become one flesh.

*Genesis 2.24**

Better is a dinner of vegetables where love is
  than a fatted ox and hatred with it.

*Proverbs 15.17**

CONFUCIANISM

The Master said: "Husband and wife should follow
    each other."

Doctrine of the Mean 15.3

When two people understand each other
    in their inmost hearts,
their words are sweet and strong,
    like the fragrance of orchids.

I Ching, Great Commentary 1.8.6

TAOISM

Cultivate harmony within your family,
    and harmony becomes fertile . . .

Tao Te Ching 54

honor your parents and respect your elders.

DO NOT DESPISE THE BREATH OF YOUR FATHERS,

BUT DRAW IT INTO YOUR BODY.

NATIVE AMERICAN RELIGIONS. *Zuni prayer*

CHRISTIANITY

Honor your father and mother,
    which is the first commandment with a promise—
that it may go well with you
    and that you may enjoy life on the earth.

Ephesians 6.2-3

Rise in the presence of the aged,
    show respect for the elderly.

Leviticus 19.32*

ISLAM

Do good to your parents.
    If either or both of them reach old age with you . . .
    speak to them with a generous word.
Lower to them the wing of humility out of mercy, and say:
My Lord, have mercy on them, as they brought me up
    when I was little.

Qur'an 17.23-24

[64]

BUDDHISM

Brethren, one can never repay two persons, I declare.
What two? Mother and father.

Anguttara Nikaya I.61

Four things increase for the one who shows
honor and respect to elders:
length of life, beauty, happiness, and health.

Dhammapada 109

HINDUISM

Let your mother be to you like unto a god!
Let your father be to you like unto a god!

Taittiriya Upanishad 1.11.2

JUDAISM

There are three partners in man: God, father, and mother.
When people honor their father and mother, God says,
"I regard it as though I had dwelt among them
and they had honored me."

Kiddushin 30b

My child, keep your father's commandment
and do not forsake your mother's teaching.

Proverbs 6.20*

CONFUCIANISM

The path of duty lies in what is near,
    and people seek for it in what is remote . . .
If each person would love his own parents
    and show the due respect to elders,
the whole land would enjoy tranquility.

Mencius IV.A.11

The noble-minded would not for all the world be stingy
    to their parents.

Mencius II.B.7

TAOISM

Fulfill your duties by your parents.

Chuang Tzu 3

Why not simply honor your parents?

Hua Hu Ching 52

love and take care of your family.

THOSE WHO HAVE RELATIVES
HARDLY TOUCH THE GROUND WHEN THEY FALL.

AFRICAN TRADITIONAL RELIGIONS. *Gbagyi proverb*

~

CHRISTIANITY

A wise woman builds her house.

Proverbs 14.1*

Fathers, do not exasperate your children.

Ephesians 6.4

Anyone who does not provide for relatives,
    and especially for immediate family,
has denied the faith.

I Timothy 5.8

ISLAM

Love your kindred.
He that does a good deed will be repaid many times over.

Qur'an 42.23

Whoever does the needful for others,
    Allah does the needful for them.

Hadith of Bukhari

[67]

Supporting one's father and mother,
  cherishing spouse and children
  and a peaceful occupation;
this is the greatest blessing.

Sutta Nipata 262

When family life possesses love and virtue,
  that is both its essence and fruition.

Tirukkural 45

He who loves his wife as himself;
  who honors her more than himself;
who rears his children in the right path,
and who marries them off at the proper time of their life,
concerning him it is written:
  "And you will know that your home is at peace."

Yebamot 62

Dwell at home in humility.

Analects 13.19

From the loving example of one family
    a whole State becomes loving,
and from its courtesies
    the whole State becomes courteous . . .
such is the nature of influence.

Great Learning, chapter 9

TAOISM

Cultivate it in yourself and virtue will become real.
Cultivate it in the family and virtue will overflow.

Tao Te Ching 54

lead with virtue and concern
for others.

GUARDIANSHIP IS NOT TO GIVE AN ORDER

BUT TO GIVE ONE'S SELF.

AFRICAN TRADITIONAL RELIGIONS. *Nyika proverb*

(Kenya and Tanzania)

CHRISTIANITY

You know that the rulers of the Gentiles lord it over them,
    and their high officials exercise authority over them.
Not so with you.
Instead, whoever wants to become great among you
    must be your servant.

Matthew 20.25-26

ISLAM

Anyone whom Allah has given the authority
    of ruling some people,
and who does not look after them in an honest manner,
    will never feel even the smell of Paradise.

Hadith of Bukhari

BUDDHISM

When cattle are crossing, if the bull goes straight,
   they all go straight because his course is straight.
So among people, if the one who's reckoned best
   lives righteously, the others do so too.
The whole land dwells in happiness if the ruler lives right.

Anguttara Nikaya II.75

HINDUISM

One is a light among rulers
   who is endowed with the four merits
   of generosity, graciousness, justice
   and care for the people.

Tirukkural 390

It is not the strength of arms that gives success to rulers,
   but their rule and its uprightness.

Tirukkural 546

JUDAISM

One who rules over people justly,
   ruling in the fear of God,
is like the light of morning,
   like the sun rising on a cloudless morning,
gleaming from the rain on the grassy land.

II Samuel 23.3-4*

CONFUCIANISM

If you govern with the power of your virtue,
    you will be like the North Star.
It just stays in its place
    while all the other stars position themselves around it.

Analects 2.1

TAOISM

All streams flow to the sea because it is lower than they are.
Humility gives it its power.
If you want to govern the people,
    you must place yourself below them.
If you want to lead the people,
    you must learn how to follow them.

Tao Te Ching 66

home altar

wherever archeologists have unearthed the remains of human civilization, they have discovered the ruins of altars. We've also learned from history that the makers of these altars shared a common understanding—that the altar is a sacred place to communicate with something or someone much greater than ourselves.

Today, in our hectic, disjointed society, the yearning to connect with Spirit runs deep. A home altar provides an intimate place where we can worship, reflect, meditate, and connect daily—it's a sacred space of our own.

SETTING UP YOUR ALTAR

Choose a place in your home that makes you feel calm, and where you can separate yourself from household bustle. Your spot may be quite ordinary, but your attitude will make it sacred.

You'll need a dedicated flat surface. This could be a small table, a shelf, a mantle, a cart, a trunk, or even a windowsill.

You may want to cover your altar with a cloth, or a piece of material that has significance for you. Whatever feels right to you is appropriate.

A home altar will usually display an eclectic mix of keepsakes—spiritual, religious, and sentimental. Think of a smattering of objects that you value, and that calm you or bring feelings of joy.

- Candles. The colors you choose could represent the focus of your worship. A white candle for purity, a yellow candle for joy, a blue candle for honesty, a green candle for healing . . .

- Sacred literature and other books that lift your spirit. You might include life-defining quotations or affirmations.

- Symbols of nature. A plant, a seashell, an autumn leaf, a beautiful stone, herbs, a flower . . .

- Crystals and gems. Most colors and shapes have significant purposes, like comfort, peace, healing, and focus.

- Statues and images. A laughing Buddha, a statue of Mary, a picture of your family. Images can serve as reminders of values and qualities you want to develop in your life.

- Earth elements—fire, water, earth, and air. Fire could be represented by a candle; water by a trickling fountain (or a bowl); earth by a rock; and air by incense.

- Nothing. An empty space could be your ideal reminder of the need to empty yourself of earthly passions and desires.

- Animal carvings. A bear may represent protection. You might see the rhythm of life in a dolphin. A hummingbird may remind you to drink the sweet nectar of life.

+ Pen and Journal—to record the spiritual guidance and insight you receive.

HOW TO WORSHIP AT YOUR ALTAR

Approach your altar, and Spirit, with humility. Whatever your bodily posture, let bowing or kneeling become the posture of your heart.

To begin, you might light a candle, burn incense, ring a bell, or say a prayer.

Saying "Thank you" for the good things in your life puts you in a positive, worshipping frame of mind.

Chanting, meditating, praying, listening, singing, and reading from a sacred text are all excellent forms of worship.

Humbly express worship by seeking guidance, asking for help for others or yourself, and sharing your private thoughts.

The word "altar," in any tradition, is inseparable from the concept of "sacrifice." Laying your will on the altar, releasing your pet resentments, giving up your anger and fear—these are the sacrifices of a humble heart.

As you close your worship, feel the qualities of compassion, integrity, and humility flowing from Spirit into your life, and out to the world.

4

from a heart of integrity

over half a lifeime of immersing myself in the various mystical traditions and in the lives of the wisest mystic teachers of these traditions, I have found that one quality—integrity—seems to characterize all sages, whatever their differences of temperament or teaching. What links Ramakrishna to Jesus to Chuang-Zu to Mother Teresa is that each was completely truthful to his or her own deepest nature, and would not betray it under any circumstances.

It is this integrity of being, this wholeness, and this ripe, unshakeable strength that make each of them fit vessels for divine revelation and inspiring examples to people of all paths. In T. S. Eliot's words, it is "a condition of complete simplicity that costs no less than everything."

How easy it is to flatter when we need something, or lie

when we have to get out of a tedious obligation. Yet we all know that when we don't follow our conscience and profoundly held beliefs, something worse than disaster or derision falls upon us: a loss of ourselves, a hemorrhage of our innermost reality that leaves us feeling empty and drained of strength and hope. We also know that when we do act from our deepest conviction, whatever the cost or consequence, a sense of peace descends on us, steadying us to endure and witness anything.

The most profound teaching about integrity that I know comes from the *Bhagavad Gita*, when Krishna tells Arjuna how it is essential for each being to do that duty prescribed to him or her by character and by destiny. He announces, "It is better for you to do your own duty, however imperfectly, than to assume the duties of another person, however successfully. Prefer to die doing your own duty; the duty of another will bring you into great spiritual danger."

This teaching of Krishna has always suggested to me that God's plan for humanity is dependent upon each person having the integrity to enact his or her own deepest nature and its laws and responsibilities in the world. The failure to do this, on the deepest level, is a betrayal of God's purpose both for oneself and the world.

Andrew Harvey

examine your motives.

WE SHOULD EXAMINE OURSELVES

AND LEARN WHAT IS THE AFFECTION AND PURPOSE OF THE HEART,

FOR IN THIS WAY ONLY CAN WE LEARN WHAT WE HONESTLY ARE.

CHRISTIAN SCIENCE. *Science and Health, p. 8*

CHRISTIANITY

The Lord will bring to light what is hidden in darkness
    and will expose the motives of the heart.

I Corinthians 4.5

The word of God is living and active.
Sharper than any double-edged sword,
    it penetrates even to dividing soul and spirit,
    joints and marrow;
it judges the thoughts and intentions of the heart.

Hebrews 4.12

ISLAM

Allah will take you to task
    for that which is intended in your hearts.

Qur'an 2.225

Actions will be judged only by intention . . .

Hadith of Bukhari

BUDDHISM

When one intends to move, or one intends to speak,
one should first examine one's own mind
    and then act appropriately with composure.
           Shantideva, A Guide to the Bodhisattva's Way of Life 5.47

If you speak or act with a corrupted heart,
    suffering follows you, as the wheel of the cart
    the track of the ox that pulls it.
           Dhammapada 1

HINDUISM

Let right deeds be your motive,
    not the fruit which comes from them.
           Bhagavad Gita 2.47

JUDAISM

The Lord searches every heart
    and understands every motive behind the thoughts.
           I Chronicles 28.9

The purposes of the heart are deep waters,
    but a person of understanding draws them out.
           Proverbs 20.5

CONFUCIANISM

The Master said: If you look at their intentions,
    examine their motives,
and scrutinize what brings them contentment—
how can people hide who they are?
    How can they hide who they really are?

Analects 2.10

If profit guides your actions,
    there will be no end of resentment.

Analects 4.12

TAOISM

Reveal your naked self and embrace your original nature;
    bind your self-interest and control your ambition . . .

Tao Te Ching 19

The wise are concerned with the depths
    and not the surface, with the fruit and not the flower.

Tao Te Ching 38

purify your heart.

ALL YOU WHO COME BEFORE ME, HOPING TO ATTAIN

THE ACCOMPLISHMENT OF YOUR DESIRES,

PRAY WITH HEARTS PURE FROM FALSEHOOD,

CLEAN WITHIN AND WITHOUT,

REFLECTING THE TRUTH LIKE A MIRROR.

SHINTO. *Oracle of Temmangu*

CHRISTIANITY

Blessed are the pure in heart, for they will see God.

Matthew 5.8

Let us purify ourselves from everything that contaminates
body and spirit.

II Corinthians 7.1

ISLAM

Know that in the body there is a bit of flesh;
when it is sound the whole body is sound,
and when it is corrupt the whole body is corrupt.
Know, it is the heart.

Hadith of Bukhari

For everything there is an appropriate way of polishing;
the heart's polishing is the remembrance of God.

Hadith of Tirmidhi

BUDDHISM

Just as silver smiths step by step, bit by bit,
    moment to moment,
blow away the impurities of molten silver—
    so the wise, their own.

Dhammapada 239

HINDUISM

Water makes external cleanliness.
    Truthfulness is the detergent of the heart.

Tirukkural 298

Just as firewood is turned to ashes in the flames of a fire,
    all actions are turned to ashes
    in wisdom's refining flames.
Nothing in the world can purify as powerfully as wisdom . . .

Bhagavad Gita 4.37-38

JUDAISM

Behold, you desire truth in the inward being;
    therefore teach me wisdom in my secret heart . . .
Create in me a clean heart, O God,
    and put a new and right spirit within me.

*Psalm 51.6, 10**

CONFUCIANISM

When chickens or dogs wander away,
    people know enough to search for them,
but when their heart wanders away they don't.
The Way of learning is nothing other than this:
    searching for the heart that's wandered away.

Mencius VI.A.11

Therefore the noble-minded examine their hearts,
    that there may be nothing wrong there.

Doctrine of the Mean 33.2

TAOISM

Can you cleanse your inner vision
    until you see nothing but the light?

Tao Te Ching 10

be honest.

SPEAK TRUTH IN HUMILITY TO ALL PEOPLE.

ONLY THEN CAN YOU BE A TRUE PERSON.

NATIVE AMERICAN RELIGIONS. *Sioux proverb*

CHRISTIANITY

Speaking the truth in love, we must grow up in every way
into him who is the head, into Christ.

Ephesians 4.15

Truthful lips endure forever,
but a lying tongue lasts only a moment.

Proverbs 12.19*

ISLAM

Bear true witness before Allah,
even though it be against yourselves . . .
do not be led by passion, or you will swerve from the truth.

Qur'an 4.135

Surely truth leads to virtue, and virtue leads to paradise,
and one continues to speak the truth
until one becomes thoroughly truthful . . .

Hadith of Bukhari

BUDDHISM

Speak the truth with discretion,
    fearlessly and in a loving heart.

Gospel of Buddha 46.7

The person who tells a lie,
    who transgresses in this one thing,
transcending concern for the world beyond:
    there's no evil he might not do.

Dhammapada 176

Lying is the origin of all evils.

Maharatnakuta Sutra 27, Bodhisattva Surata's Discourse

HINDUISM

Speaking the truth with kindness,
    honesty that causes no pain . . .
this is control of speech.

Bhagavad Gita 17.15

The one who is dishonest with respect to speech
    is dishonest in everything.

Laws of Manu 4.256

The speech of enlightened ones
    consists of truth soaked in affection . . .
find the words that save truth from harshness.

Tirukkural 91, 96

JUDAISM

The seal of God is truth.

Shabbat 55

Buy the truth and do not sell it;
   get wisdom, discipline, and understanding.

Proverbs 23.23*

Whoever of you loves life
   and desires to see many good days,
keep your tongue from evil
   and your lips from speaking lies.

Psalm 34.12-13*

CONFUCIANISM

The object of the superior person is truth.

Analects 15.31

Confucius said, "I do not see what use
   a person can be put to,
whose word cannot be trusted."

Analects 2.22

TAOISM

In speech, sincerity guides the person of Tao.

Tao Te Ching 8

Do not assert with your mouth what your heart denies.

Tract of the Quiet Way

be trustworthy.

CHRISTIANITY

Whoever can be trusted with very little
    can also be trusted with much,
and whoever is dishonest with very little
    will also be dishonest with much.
If you have not been trustworthy
    in handling worldly wealth,
who will trust you with true riches?

Luke 16.10-11

Like a bad tooth or a lame foot is reliance on the unfaithful
    in times of trouble.

Proverbs 25.19*

ISLAM

Keep your promises;
    you are accountable for all that you promise.

Qur'an 17.34

Those that sell . . . their own oaths for a paltry price
    will have no share in the world to come.

Qur'an 3.77

BUDDHISM

Keep company with the trustworthy—
they will make you happy like close family.

Dhammapada 207

[A bhikkhu] is trustworthy, reliable,
    and undeceiving of the world.

The Noble Eightfold Path

HINDUISM

Let no wise person swear an oath falsely,
    even in a trifling matter;
for whoever swears an oath falsely is lost in this world
    and after death.

Laws of Manu 8.111

JUDAISM

It is better not to vow than to make a vow and not fulfill it.
Do not let your mouth lead you into sin.

Ecclesiastes 5.5-6*

Let love and faithfulness never leave you;
    bind them around your neck,
    write them on the tablet of your heart.
Then you will win favor and a good name
    in the sight of God and of people.

Proverbs 3.3-4*

CONFUCIANISM

The Master's teaching all hangs on faithfulness
and fellow-feeling.

Analects 4.15

Without trust a people cannot stand.

Analects 12.7

TAOISM

Whoever lightly makes a promise
will find it often hard to keep their faith.
Whoever makes light of many things
will encounter many difficulties.

Tao Te Ching 63

don't steal.

Stolen food never satisfies hunger.

NATIVE AMERICAN RELIGIONS. *Omaha proverb*

CHRISTIANITY

Thieves must give up stealing;
rather let them labor and work honestly
  with their own hands,
so as to have something to share with the needy.

Ephesians 4.28

ISLAM

You shall not take each other's money illicitly,
nor shall you bribe the officials to deprive others
  of some of their rights illicitly, while you know.

Qur'an 2.188

BUDDHISM

Whoever takes by theft what has not been given to them,
  and what is cherished by others,
should be known as an outcast.

Sutta Nipata 119

HINDUISM

The mere thought of sin is sin.
Therefore, avoid even the thought of stealing from another.

Tirukkural 282

The wickedness of evil-minded thieves,
　　who secretly prowl over this earth,
cannot be restrained except by punishment.

Laws of Manu 9.263

JUDAISM

Ill-gotten treasures are of no value.

Proverbs 10.2*

You shall not steal.

Exodus 20.15*

CONFUCIANISM

Virtue is the "root" and wealth is the "branches."
　　Wealth taken wrongly will also leave wrongly.

The Great Learning, chapter 10

Those who seize property are like those
    who relieve their hunger by eating tainted meat,
    or quench their thirst by drinking poisoned liquor.

Treatise on Response & Retribution 5

There are some people whose behavior is unrighteous . . .
They impoverish others for their own gain . . .
They break into others' houses
    to take their property and valuables.

Treatise on Response & Retribution 3

don't commit adultery.

VIOLATING AND MISUSING LOVE

IS THE GRAVEST OF ALL CRIMES.

UNIFICATION CHURCH. *Sun Myung Moon, 3/20/77*

CHRISTIANITY

Guard yourself in your spirit,
  and do not break faith with the wife of your youth.

Malachi 2.15*

Can fire be carried in the bosom
  without burning one's clothes?
Anyone who commits adultery lacks judgment.

Proverbs 6.27, 32*

ISLAM

Don't come nigh to adultery:
  for it is a shameful deed and an evil,
opening the road to other evils.

Qur'an 17.32

Four misfortunes befall a careless person
    who commits adultery:
acquisition of demerit, disturbed sleep, blame,
    and a state of woe.
There is acquisition of demerit as well as evil destiny.

Dhammapada 309

HINDUISM

"Let mutual fidelity continue until death,"
this may be considered as the summary of the highest law
    for husband and wife.

Laws of Manu 9.101

A man should not think incontinently of another's wife,
    much less address her to that end;
for such a man will be reborn in a future life
    as a creeping insect.
Whoever commits adultery is punished both here
    and hereafter.

Vishnu Purana 3.11

JUDAISM

Drink water from your own cistern,
    flowing water from your own well.
Let your fountain be blessed,
    and rejoice in the wife of your youth . . .
be intoxicated always by her love.

*Proverbs 5.15-19**

You shall not commit adultery.

Exodus 20.14*

CONFUCIANISM

Don't do what shouldn't be done
and don't desire what shouldn't be desired.
That's all there is to it.

Mencius VII.A.17

TAOISM

Do not approach your neighbor's wife or maids.

Tract of the Quiet Way

It is true that you commit no actual crimes;
but when you meet a beautiful woman in another's home
and cannot banish her from your thoughts,
you have committed adultery with her in your heart.

Treatise on Response & Retribution, Moral Tales 12

practice what you preach.

THEY SAY ONE THING, AND DO SOMETHING ELSE.

THERE IS NO LOVE IN THEIR HEARTS,

AND YET WITH THEIR MOUTHS THEY TALK TALL.

SIKHISM. *Guru Granth Sahib, Gauri Sukhmani, p. 269*

CHRISTIANITY

They do not practice what they teach.
They tie up heavy burdens, hard to bear,
    and lay them on the shoulders of others;
but they themselves are unwilling to lift a finger
    to move them.
They do all their deeds to be seen by others.

Matthew 23.3-5

Let us love, not in word or speech, but in truth and action.

I John 3.18

ISLAM

It is most hateful in the sight of Allah
    that you say that which you do not.

Qur'an 61.3

That knowledge is very superficial
    which remains only on your tongue:
the intrinsic merit and value of knowledge
    is that you act up to it.

Shiite. *Nahjul Balaga, saying 93*

BUDDHISM

Whatever advice you give to others, do the same yourself.

Dhammapada 159

As a flower that is lovely and beautiful, but is scentless,
even so fruitless is the well-spoken word
    of one who does not practice it.

Dhammapada 51

HINDUISM

There are no bigger fools than those
    who have acquired much learning
and preach the same to others,
    but who do not control themselves.

Tirukkural 834

JUDAISM

Say little and do much.

The Fathers According to Rabbi Nathan XXIII.I

The other rivers say to the Euphrates, "How come you
   don't sound off as you flow, the way in which the rest
   of us make our flow heard from a distance?"
The river said to them, "My deeds give evidence
   concerning me, so I don't have to announce
   how great I am."

Sifre Deuteronomy VI.III.3

CONFUCIANISM

The noble-minded are ashamed
   if their words outshine their actions.

Analects 14.29

TAOISM

The wise don't talk, they act.

Tao Te Ching 17

don't be a hypocrite.

DISPENSE WITH SAP-WOOD, LET ONLY THE HEART-WOOD STAND.

NEW ZEALAND TRADITIONAL RELIGION. *Maori proverb*

CHRISTIANITY

You hypocrites! You are like whitewashed tombs,
    which look beautiful on the outside,
but on the inside are full of dead men's bones . . .
On the outside you appear to people as righteous,
but on the inside you are full of hypocrisy and wickedness.

Matthew 23.27-28

ISLAM

The hypocrites are afraid . . .
    Allah will surely bring to light what they are dreading.

Qur'an 9.64

The hypocrites are surely in the lowest depths of the fire
    . . . except for those who repent and amend
    and hold fast to Allah—
these are with the believers.
And Allah will soon grant the believers a mighty reward.

Qur'an 4.145-146

BUDDHISM

Mistaking the false for the true and the true for the false
you overlook the heart and fill yourself with desire.
See the false as false and the true as true.
Look into your heart. Follow your nature.

Dhammapada 11-12

The tangle's inside you.
You comb the outside.

Dhammapada 394

HINDUISM

They know not purity nor right behavior,
    they possess no truthfulness . . .
They are full of hypocrisy.

Bhagavad Gita 16.17

Of what avail is an outer appearance of saintliness,
if the mind suffers inwardly from knowledge of
    its iniquity?

Tirukkural 272

JUDAISM

These people come near to me with their mouths
    and honor me with their lips,
but their hearts are far from me.

*Isaiah 29.13**

With their lips they show much love,
    but their heart is set on their gain.

*Ezekiel 33.31**

CONFUCIANISM

Fine words and an insinuating appearance
  are seldom associated with true virtue.

Analects 1.3

TAOISM

When the great way falls into disuse . . .
  When cleverness emerges,
there is great hypocrisy.

Tao Te Ching 18

⁓

cultivate a strong work ethic.

IF YOU CARRY THE EGG BASKET DO NOT DANCE.

AFRICAN TRADITIONAL RELIGIONS. *Ambede proverb*

CHRISTIANITY

Whatever you do, work at it with all your heart,
    as working for the Lord, not for your employer.

Colossians 3.23

Everyone should test their own work.
Then they can take pride in themselves,
    without comparing themselves to others,
for everyone should carry their own load.

Galatians 6.4-5

ISLAM

No one eats better food
    than that which one eats out of the work
    of one's own hand.

Hadith of Bukhari

BUDDHISM

Skillful and vigorous one should always do the work
oneself.
With respect to all works, one should not leave
the opportunity to someone else.

A Guide to the Boddhisattva Way of Life 5.82

HINDUISM

There is no dish so sweet as that earned by one's own labor,
be it but the thinnest gruel.

Tirukkural 1065

Good people put forth industry and produce wealth,
not for themselves but for the use of society.

Tirukkural 212

JUDAISM

Go to the ant, you sluggard; consider its ways and be wise!
It has no commander, no overseer or ruler,
yet it stores its provisions in summer
and gathers its food at harvest.

Proverbs 6.6-8*

Whatever your hand finds to do, do it with all your might.

Ecclesiastes 9.10*

CONFUCIANISM

When asked, "What is love?" The Master said:
"To be respectful at home, painstaking at work,
faithful to all."

Analects 13.19

The wise work diligently without allegiance to words.
They teach by doing, not by saying;
 are genuinely helpful, not discriminating;
 are positive, not possessive.
They do not proclaim their accomplishments,
 and because they do not proclaim them,
 credit for them can never be taken away.

Tao Te Ching 2

sacred reading

every major tradition has at least one sacred text. Adherents read, study, memorize, chant, reflect on, and even sing the divinely inspired words of their canon. And there's a good reason for this: Sacred literature holds the secrets of eternal life, nirvana, enlightenment, joy, and peace.

Scriptures also provide a moral and spiritual touchstone to test the genuineness of our character.

Islamic Tafakkur means to reflect on a subject deeply. But the meaning goes even further; this reflection allows the follower to discern between good and evil—it is the heart's lamp and the spirit's food.

Hinduism tells us to read the sutras not as an intellectual exercise, but to read, meditate, and reflect upon them. In this way, our character is deeply affected and transformed.

Christianity agrees. "Lectio Divina," literally "Divine Reading," is an ancient art that is gaining renewed momentum today. This practice involves reading scripture, or more accurately, listening to it—with our hearts. We can apply this exercise to any passage of any sacred text.

LECTIO DIVINA

Before you begin, find a quiet place where you can calm your spirit. If you are to hear Spirit's gentle voice, you must be quiet, outside and in.

SPIRITUAL PRACTICE

1. Reading ("Lectio"). Read slowly, pausing to ponder and reflect. Read the passage several times. Read attentively, listening with the ear of your heart.

2. Meditation ("Meditatio"). When a word or phrase impresses you deeply, stay with it. Chew on it, memorize it, repeat it to yourself, own it. This is Spirit's word for you.

3. Prayer ("Oratio"). Leave your thinking behind, and let your heart respond to the inspiration you received. You may feel prompted to confess, offer praise, or release a problem. Talk to Spirit, and allow the word to shine its light into the recesses of your heart. Let it change you at the deepest level.

4. Contemplation ("Contemplatio"). There are times in every meaningful relationship when words are needless. Sit back and enjoy the silent companionship of Spirit.

Through this practice we discover an underlying spiritual rhythm. A natural cadence that swings between activity and receptivity.

Activity speaks of an inward working on our character and behavior. We examine our motives. We hold ourselves up to the touchstone of scripture. We make resolutions. We change.

Then we swing to receptivity, and we cease all doing. We contemplate. We rest. We simply be.

Both are needful to maintain balance—and to live a lifetime of integrity.

5

from a heart of faith

during one of the darkest times of my life, I learned three important lessons about faith—that it was the oxygen of survival; that without it, the suffering of trying to do God's will would be unendurable; and that it brings in the end not only true divine protection, but a flowering of all possible joys, inner and outer.

I am grateful that I know beyond a shadow of a doubt that the three powers of faith are real, because I meet many people whose faith is wavering, ambiguous, or even nonexistent. So to speak to them not from the authority of the Scriptures but from the depths of personal experience—about what happens when you truly hold on in faith to the Divine—allows me to bring hope where there has been despair, and light where there has been darkness. In the end, however, I have found that words about faith can help only a little; what really helps another person—and not immediately, either, but in the long run—is trying to show them what a life lived in, with, and for faith looks like.

This has never been more important than now. I think of this time as presenting humanity with what St. John of the Cross has called "the dark night of the soul" and what Matthew Fox speaks of as "the dark night of the species." In such difficult times, it is easy to lose faith and to believe that history is meaningless or that God has abandoned us to our devices. What authentic faith keeps alive for oneself and for others is the strength to go on loving and hoping, come what may, and the power to root oneself in the calm of your eternal nature while risking everything to fulfill your human responsibilities.

Pythagoras wrote, "Have faith, for human nature is divine." Having faith in the inherent "divinity" of human nature—which all the mystical traditions testify to—is how I have kept believing in the future of humanity, and its ability to change and transform in time.

Andrew Harvey

believe your body is temporary,
your spirit immortal.

SO LONG AS YOU REMAIN UNKNOWING THAT THE BODY

IS A THING BORROWED,

YOU CAN UNDERSTAND NOTHING AT ALL.

TENRIKYO. *Ofudesaki III.137*

CHRISTIANITY

Our citizenship is in heaven.

Philippians 3.20

The body that is sown is perishable, it is raised imperishable;
it is sown in dishonor, it is raised in glory;
it is sown in weakness, it is raised in power;
it is sown a natural body, it is raised a spiritual body.

I Corinthians 15.42-44

ISLAM

Now no person knows what delights of the eye
are kept hidden in reserve for them—
as a reward for their good deeds.

Qur'an 32.17

Be in the world as if you were a stranger or a traveler.

Forty Hadith of an-Nawawi 40

BUDDHISM

Look upon the world as a bubble,
    look upon it as a mirage:
the king of death does not see the one
    who thus looks down upon the world.

Dhammapada 170

Whoever follows the right path has joy in this world
    and in the world beyond.

Dhammapada 168

HINDUISM

The soul's connection with the body
    is just that of the bird's with the eggshell.
The bird leaves it joyfully to fly in the air.

Tirukkural 338

As rivers flowing into the ocean find their final peace,
    and their name and form disappear,
even so the wise become free from name and form
and enter into the radiance of the Supreme Spirit
    who is greater than all greatness.

Mundaka Upanishad 3.2.8

JUDAISM

The body is the sheath of the soul.

Sanhedrin 108a

The dust returns to the ground it came from,
    and the spirit returns to God who gave it.

*Ecclesiastes 12.7**

In the way of righteousness there is life;
    along that path there is immortality.

*Proverbs 12.28**

CONFUCIANISM

All the living must die, and dying, return to the ground;
    this is what is called kuei.
The bones and flesh molder below, and, hidden away,
    become the earth of the fields.
But the spirit issues forth, and is displayed on high
    in a condition of glorious brightness.

Book of Ritual 21.2.1

TAOISM

Those who are at one with the Tao abide forever.
Even after their bodies waste away, they are safe and whole.

Tao Te Ching 16

By and by comes the great awakening;
    then we find that this life is really a great dream.

Chuang Tzu 2

live without fear of death.

SO LIVE YOUR LIFE

SO THE FEAR OF DEATH CAN NEVER ENTER YOUR HEART.

NATIVE AMERICAN RELIGIONS. *Tecumseh, Shawnee proverb*

CHRISTIANITY

For to me, living is Christ and dying is gain.

Philippians 1.21

That by his own death,
Jesus might destroy him who holds the power of
    death—that is, the devil—
and free those who all their lives were held in slavery
    by their fear of death.

Hebrews 2.14-15

ISLAM

When the time of the death of believers approaches,
they receive the good news of Allah's pleasure with them
    and His blessings upon them,
and so at that time nothing is dearer to them
    than what is in front of them.
They therefore love the meeting with Allah,
    and Allah loves the meeting with them.

Hadith of Bukhari

BUDDHISM

If you have given up bad conduct
in deeds, speech, and thought
and have cultivated good conduct
in deeds, speech, and thought;
if you have given up wrong view and cultivated right view,
you need not fear death.

Anguttara Nikaya IV.116

HINDUISM

The virtuous saints never fear death
and the state after death.

Matsya Purana 212.25

If you place a gulf between yourself and God,
this gulf will bring fear.
But if you find the support of the Invisible and Ineffable,
you are free from fear.

Taittiriya Upanishad 2.7

JUDAISM

Holy ones exult in glory, they sing for joy on their beds
(Ps. 149.5):
"In what glory will they exult?
It is in the glory that the Holy One, blessed be he,
does with the righteous
when they take their leave of the world."

Pesiqta Rabbati II.III.2

CONFUCIANISM

My Integrity is born of Heaven.
So what can Huan T'ui's assassins do to me?

Analects 7.23

If, on self-examination, I find that I am not upright,
will I not fear even a poor man
in loose garments of haircloth?
If, on self-examination, I find that I am upright,
I will go forward against thousands and tens of thousands.

Mencius II.A.2

TAOISM

You hold nothing back from life;
therefore you are ready for death,
as a person is ready for sleep after a good day's work.

Tao Te Ching 50

How do I know but that he who dreads death is not as a child
who has lost his way and does not know his way home?

Chuang Tzu 2

know that truth is eternal, unchanging.

NOTHING IS REAL BUT THE ETERNAL.

NOTHING WILL LAST BUT THE ETERNAL.

SIKHISM. *Guru Granth Sahib, Japuji 1, p. 1*

CHRISTIANITY

In the beginning was the Word,
    and the Word was with God, and the Word was God.
He was with God in the beginning.
Through him all things were made.

John 1.1-3

All your words are true; all your righteous laws are eternal.

Psalm 119.160*

ISLAM

The Words of Allah will never change.

Qur'an 10.64

You will find no change in the way of Allah.

Qur'an 33.62

BUDDHISM

Truth knows neither birth nor death;
    it has no beginning and no end.
Welcome the truth.
    The truth is the immortal part of mind.
Establish the truth in your mind,
    for the truth is the image of the eternal;
it portrays the immutable; it reveals the everlasting;
    the truth gives unto mortals the boon of immortality.

Gospel of Buddha 2.10

HINDUISM

This, in the beginning, was the only Lord of the Universe.
    His Word was with him.
This Word was his second. He contemplated. He said,
"I will deliver this Word so that she will produce
    and bring into being all this world."

Tandya Maha Brahmana 20.14.2

Whoever has realized eternal Truth does not see death . . .

Chandogya Upanishad 7.27

JUDAISM

I [wisdom] was appointed from eternity,
    from the beginning,
    before the world began.
I was there when he set the heavens in place . . .
Then I was the craftsman at his side.

Proverbs 8.23, 27, 30

Surely the people are grass.
The grass withers and the flowers fall,
　　but the word of our God stands forever.

CONFUCIANISM

Absolute Truth is indestructible.
　　Being indestructible, it is eternal.
Being eternal, it is self-existent.
　　Being self-existent, it is infinite.
Being infinite, it is vast and deep.
Being vast and deep, it is transcendental and intelligent.

Doctrine of the Mean 26.1-3

TAOISM

The Truth is that which is received from Heaven.
By nature it is the way it is and cannot be changed.

Chuang Tzu 31

acknowledge an all-knowing presence.

THERE IS NOT A SINGLE PLACE IN ALL THE CORNERS OF THE
WORLD WHERE GOD IS ABSENT.

OMOTO KYO. *Michi-no-Shiori*

CHRISTIANITY

Nothing in all creation is hidden from God's sight.

Hebrews 4.13

"Am I only a God nearby," declares the Lord,
    "and not a God far away?
Can anyone hide in secret places so that I cannot see him?"
    declares the Lord.
"Do I not fill heaven and earth?"

Jeremiah 23.24*

ISLAM

Whichever way you turn there is the face of Allah.
    Allah is omnipresent and all-knowing.

Qur'an 2.115

With Allah are the treasures of the unseen—
    none knows them but he.

And he knows what is in the land and the sea.
And there falls not a leaf but he knows it.

Qur'an 6.59

BUDDHISM

I am one who knows all things, sees all things.

Lotus Sutra, chapter 5

Always I am aware of which living beings practice the way,
and which do not.

Lotus Sutra, chapter 16

HINDUISM

The great Ruler of all these worlds,
beholds as if from near at hand
the man who thinks he acts by stealth.

Atharva Veda 4.16.1

He is everlasting and omnipresent,
infinite in the great and infinite in the small.

Mundaka Upanishad 1.1.6

He is the Spirit that is in all things.

Mundaka Upanishad 2.1.4

JUDAISM

Mark well three things
and you will not fall into the clutches of sin:
know what is above you—
an eye that sees, an ear that hears,
and all your actions recorded in the book.

Abot 2.1

The eyes of the Lord are everywhere,
keeping watch on the wicked and the good.

*Proverbs 15.3**

Great Heaven is clear-seeing,
and is with you in your wanderings and indulgences.

Book of Songs, Ode 254

Although a fish sink and lie at the bottom,
it is still quite clearly seen.

Doctrine of the Mean 33.2

Oh, unfathomable source of all things! . . .
Hidden deep but ever present!

Tao Te Ching 4

We look at it, and see it not; though it is Omnipresent;
and we name it the Root-Balance.
We listen for it, and hear it not, though it is Omniscient;
and we name it the Silence.
We feel for it, and touch it not, though it is Omnipotent;
and we name it the Concealed.

Tao Te Ching 14

~

seek and you will find.

UNLESS YOU CALL OUT, WHO WILL OPEN THE DOOR?

AFRICAN TRADITIONAL RELIGIONS. *Ethiopian proverb*

CHRISTIANITY

Ask and it will be given to you;
search and you will find;
knock and the door will be opened for you.

Matthew 7.7

ISLAM

If you are mindful of Allah, you will find him before you.
When you ask for anything, ask it from Allah,
and if you seek help, seek help in Allah.

Hadith of Tirmidhi

Allah said . . . If anyone comes to me walking,
I will come to him at a run.

Hadith of Muslim

BUDDHISM

The Buddha will pour down the rain of the Dharma
fulfilling those that seek the path of enlightenment.

Lotus Sutra, chapter 1

God is found in the soul
    when sought with truth and self-sacrifice,
as fire is found in wood, water in hidden springs,
    cream in milk, and oil in the oil-fruit.

Svetasvatara Upanishad 1.15

Concentrate your mind on me,
    fill your heart with my presence,
love me, serve me, worship me,
    and you will attain me at last.

Bhagavad Gita 9.34

JUDAISM

When you search for me, you will find me;
    if you seek me with all your heart.

Jeremiah 29.13*

Serve God with wholehearted devotion
    and with a willing mind . . .
If you seek him, he will be found by you.

I Chronicles 28.9*

CONFUCIANISM

What you seek you will find,
    and what you ignore you will lose.

Mencius VII.A.3

Why do people value the Tao?
Is it not because through it you can find what you seek,
  and because of it you can escape
  what is hounding you?
Therefore, it is the most valuable thing under heaven.

Tao Te Ching 62

recognize a loving, universal Parent

ALL OF YOU IN THE WORLD ARE MY CHILDREN. LOVE OF YOU

FILLS ME: THIS IS MY SINGLE HEART.

TENRIKYO. *Ofudesaki XVII.16*

CHRISTIANITY

The Spirit himself testifies with our spirit
that we are God's children.

Romans 8.16

Jesus said . . . "I am returning to my Father and your Father,
to my God and your God."

John 20.17

As a mother comforts her child, so I will comfort you.

Isaiah 66.13*

ISLAM

All creatures are Allah's children,
and those dearest to Allah
are those who treat His children kindly.

Hadith of Baihaqi

Verily I am beside you, as a father is beside his children.

Hadith of Abu Dawud

BUDDHISM

The "Thus Come One" is a father to all the world . . .
his great pity and great compassion
   are constant and unflagging;
at all times he seeks what is good and will bring benefit to all.

Lotus Sutra, chapter 3

HINDUISM

I am the father of this universe, the mother . . .
   I am that which is and that which is not.

Bhagavad Gita 9.18

God! Give us wisdom as a father gives to his sons.

Rig Veda 7.32.26

That breast of yours which is inexhaustible, health-giving . . .
   lay that bare, Sarasvati [divine Mother], for our nurture.

Rig Veda 1.164.49

JUDAISM

O Lord, you are our Father.
We are the clay, you are the potter;
   we are all the work of your hand.

Isaiah 64.8*

My child, do not despise the Lord's discipline
   and do not resent his rebuke,
because the Lord disciplines those he loves,
   as a father the child he delights in.

Proverbs 3.11*

CONFUCIANISM

Heaven and Earth are the father and mother
of the ten thousand things.

Book of History 5.1.1: The Great Declaration

TAOISM

The Tao is called the Great Mother.

Tao Te Ching 6

True people simply look upon God as their father;
if they love him with what is born of the body,
will they not love him also
with that which is greater than the body?

Chuang Tzu 6

communicate through prayer or worship.

ALMIGHTY GOD,

THE GREAT THUMB WE CANNOT EVADE

TO TIE ANY KNOT . . .

YOU ARE THE ONE WHO DOES NOT HESITATE

TO RESPOND TO OUR CALL.

AFRICAN TRADITIONAL RELIGIONS.

Native African Prayer for Peace

CHRISTIANITY

The eyes of the Lord are on the righteous
and his ears are attentive to their prayers.

I Peter 3.12

When you pray, go into your room, close the door
and pray to your Father, who is unseen.
Then your Father, who sees what is done in secret,
will reward you.

Matthew 6.5

Extol the Lord our God; worship at his footstool. Holy is he!
Psalm 99.5*

ISLAM

Call on your Lord humbly and in secret.

Qur'an 7.55

Seek assistance through patience and prayer.

Qur'an 2.45

We take on Allah's own dye.
    And who has a better dye than our Lord?
Him will we worship.

Qur'an 2.138

BUDDHISM

I fully acknowledge all negative actions
    and rejoice in all merit.
I prostrate to all the buddhas.
    May I attain supreme primordial wisdom.

The Aspiration Prayer of Maitreya–Ratnakuta, Sutra, chapter 41

With a joyful mind
    sing a song in praise of the Buddha's virtue.

Lotus Sutra, chapter 2

HINDUISM

My inner armor is prayer.

Rig Veda 6.75.19

When you have let go of attachments,
when your mind is rooted in wisdom,
    everything you do is worship.

Bhagavad Gita 4.23

JUDAISM

Come, let us bow down in worship,
    let us kneel before the Lord our Maker;
for he is our God and we are the people of his pasture,
    the flock under his care.

Psalm 95.6-7*

Let everything that breathes praise the Lord!

Psalm 150.6*

The prayers of people are heard
    only if they make their hearts as soft as flesh.

Sotah 5a-b

CONFUCIANISM

If you offend Heaven, there is no one you can pray to.

Analects 3.13

TAOISM

Take time to . . . worship the unnameable.

Hua Hu Ching 81

—

accept the existence of spiritual beings.

THE SPIRITS OF MY ANCESTORS

HAVE LOOKED DOWN FROM HEAVEN,

WATCHING OVER AND HELPING ME.

SHINTOISM. *Nihon Shoki 3*

CHRISTIANITY

Are not all angels ministering spirits
    sent to serve those who will inherit salvation?

Hebrews 1.14

ISLAM

Praise be to Allah . . . the maker of the angels,
    messengers flying on wings.

Qur'an 35.1

BUDDHISM

Heavenly beings made music, a hundred, a thousand,
    ten thousand varieties,
all at the same time in the midst of the air.

Lotus Sutra, chapter 3

The heavenly beings day and night for the sake of the Law
constantly guard and protect them.

Lotus Sutra, chapter 14

HINDUISM

Blessed is human birth;
    even the dwellers in heaven desire this birth:
for true wisdom and pure love may be attained only by man.

Bhagavata Purana 11.13

JUDAISM

If you make the Most High your dwelling . . .
he will command his angels concerning you,
    to guard you in all your ways.

Psalm 91.9, 11*

CONFUCIANISM

Confucius said, "The overabundance of the power
    of spiritual beings is truly amazing!
Looking for them, they cannot be seen.
Listening for them, they cannot be heard.
    There is nothing that they do not embody."

Doctrine of the Mean 16.1-2

TAOISM

The person of kingly virtue moves in simplicity . . .
Taking a stand in the original source,
    such a one's understanding extends to the spirits.

Chuang Tzu 12

SPIRITUAL PRACTICE

worship through song, dance, and chant

some people enjoy quiet, reverent worship. Others involve their entire body while making as much noise as humanly possible. How we worship is a personal choice, and we don't need to stifle our creative worshipping urges. Dancing, singing, chanting, shouting, clapping, drum-beating, tambourine jangling, and instrument strumming are woven intermittently throughout the fabric of just about every major faith.

The desire to unite with Spirit through voice and dance spans history and geography. Bhagavad Gita, the Hindu sacred text, means "Song of the Lord." The Psalms were originally sung and occasionally even danced by King David. From the Native American Sun Dance to the Tibetan Buddhist Dharma Protector Dance to the Sufi whirling dervish, to the Catholic Gregorian Chant and the Muslim recitation of the Qur'an with tajwid, followers express their devotion actively and loudly. Even Confucius recognized the importance of music and dance.

Expressions in worship range from spontaneous individual praise to choreographed dramatic presentation to congregational celebration of Spirit's love. As individuals, we feel physically unshackled when we twirl and lift our arms or sing at the top of our lungs. Our release is even deeper when we direct our song and movement to Spirit. It's about letting go and releasing our spirits to soar with Spirit.

SPIRITUAL PRACTICE

Dance meditation is another means of individual expression. When we pray, we talk to Spirit; when we meditate, we listen. And so it is with dance meditation. Listening to Spirit is a true form of worship, acknowledging that what Spirit says is of greater value than any words we could offer. As we relax and move about, we become receptive to Spirit's voice.

As observers, when we view a sacred dance or song performance, we are stirred to tears and enveloped with joy. In our hearts we worship right along with the performers.

As a group, vocal harmony and synchronized movement unify us by powerfully and beautifully blending together lifestyles, shapes, ages, and colors.

Faith is three-dimensional; our worship can be, too.

EXPRESSING YOURSELF THROUGH WORSHIP

Sing your own prayers of entreaty and gratitude.
Beat a drum with sticks that represent greed,
anger, and ignorance.
Recite with feeling a meaningful passage.
Dance the spiritual stories that you love.
Sing your favorite scripture.
Close your eyes and wave your arms before Spirit.
Chant a powerful mantra.
Stretch your hands toward heaven—reaching—
then bend humbly toward the floor.
Make a joyful noise!
Dance while you meditate and listen to Spirit.
Don't focus outwardly on form and technique—
simply allow Spirit to guide you.

6

from a
heart of
wisdom

i had the joy of interviewing the Dalai Lama in Oslo in 1989, on the day before he was awarded the Nobel Peace Prize. We had a marvelous hour-long conversation that danced through a variety of topics—Tibet, nonviolence, the future of the world—and just before our time was up, I asked him:

"What for you is wisdom?"

He laughed. "We have only five minutes left and you ask me this?"

Then he leaned back in his chair, closed his eyes, seemed to concentrate his whole being and began:

"For me, as a Buddhist monk, the highest wisdom is to understand the empty nature of all things, beings, thoughts, and activities. All these are transient and arise interdependently with each other. Knowing this frees your whole being into the infinite spacious freedom of your Buddha-nature, which is like a cloudless sky, and from that knowledge, compassion and altruism radiate like beams from a sun.

"In more humble terms, I would say that wisdom has for me four essential faces. One face—and this is very important—is discrimination. Without the capacity to discriminate between what is real or unreal, true or false, helpful or hurtful, creative or destructive, you are lost. Discrimination is usually won not merely by meditation but through the difficulties of experience.

"The second face that wisdom wears for me is that of patience, really to be wise without bitterness or regret. Often in this life you must wait a very long time for what you pray for to happen."

"And what for you is the third face?"

"To avoid anything that causes pain or difficulty to others because inevitably, by the law of Karma, it will rebound on you and you will suffer."

"And the fourth?"

Here he leaned forward and grabbed both my hands in his. "To be joyful," he laughed again with his unmistakable laugh. "To always try to give and receive joy in whatever circumstances you find yourself! A truly wise man has an inner joy that is like a fire; it warms the world."

Gazing deep into his tender and brilliant eyes, I knew what he meant.

Andrew Harvey

know that you are accountable
for your actions.

DO NOT LOOK WHERE YOU FELL, BUT WHERE YOU SLIPPED.

AFRICAN TRADITIONAL RELIGIONS. *Liberian proverb*

CHRISTIANITY

Everything is uncovered and laid bare
before the eyes of him to whom we must give account.

Hebrews 4.13

You may be sure that your sin will find you out.

Numbers 32.23*

ISLAM

You are accountable for none but yourself.

Qur'an 4.84

It is but your deeds that I reckon up for you
and then recompense you for,
so let those who find good, praise Allah;
and let those who find other than that,
blame no one but themselves.

Forty Hadith of an-Nawawi 23

BUDDHISM

By oneself the evil is done,
by oneself one suffers;
by oneself evil is left undone,
by oneself one is purified.
Purity and impurity depend on oneself,
    no one can purify another.

Dhammapada 165

HINDUISM

Single is each being born; single it dies;
single it enjoys the reward of its virtue;
single it suffers the punishment of its sin.

Laws of Manu 4.240

JUDAISM

(1) Despite your wishes were you formed,
(2) despite your wishes were you born,
(3) despite your wishes you live,
(4) despite your wishes do you die, and
(5) despite your wishes are you going to give a
    full accounting before the King of kings of kings,
    the Holy One, blessed be he.

Abot 4.22

CONFUCIANISM

To despise disgrace and yet practice Inhumanity—
that's like despising water and living in bottomlands . . .
We bring it all upon ourselves: prosperity and ruin alike.

Mencius II.A.4

TAOISM

Heaven's net is vast. It is loose.
Yet nothing slips through.

Tao Te Ching 73

accept that you reap what you sow.

THE BODY IS THE FIELD OF ACTION . . .

AS YOU PLANT, SO WILL YOU HARVEST.

SIKHISM. *Guru Granth Sahib, Gauri Var, p. 308*

CHRISTIANITY

You reap what you sow . . .
if you sow to please the Spirit,
    from the Spirit you will reap eternal life.

Galatians 6.7-8

Whoever sows sparingly will also reap sparingly,
    and whoever sows generously will also reap generously.

II Corinthians 9.6

ISLAM

Good is the reward for those who do good in this world.

Qur'an 39.10

BUDDHISM

Do not think lightly of good
    that not the least consequence will come of it.
A whole waterpot will fill up from dripping drops of water.
The wise fill themselves with good, just a little at a time.

Dhammapada 121-122

HINDUISM

Good conduct sows good,
    and from bad springs eternal trouble.

Tirukkural 138

JUDAISM

Whoever sows righteousness reaps a sure reward.

Proverbs 11.18*

CONFUCIANISM

Whatever you give out is given back.

Mencius I.B.12

TAOISM

Curses and blessings do not come through gates,
    but people themselves invite their arrival.
The reward of good and evil
    is like the shadow accompanying a body,
and so it is apparent that heaven and earth are possessed
    of crime-recording spirits.

Treatise on Response & Retribution, Introduction

learn the difference between right and wrong.

DO WHAT YOU KNOW TO BE RIGHT.

NATIVE AMERICAN RELIGIONS.

From the Native American Commandments

CHRISTIANITY

You need milk, not solid food!
    Anyone who lives on milk, being still an infant,
    is not acquainted with the teaching
    about righteousness.
But solid food is for the mature,
    who by constant use have trained themselves
    to distinguish good from evil.

Hebrews 5.13-14

Hate what is evil; cling to what is good.

Romans 12.9

ISLAM

Who will lose most through their works?
Those whose deeds in this world are misguided
    and who yet think that what they do is right. . . .

Qur'an 18.103-104

Virtue is that by which the soul enjoys repose
and the heart tranquility.
Sin is what introduces trouble into the soul.

Forty Hadith of an-Nawawi 27

BUDDHISM

One who clearly ascertains both right and wrong
is the one who is held as wise.

Dhammapada 256

A person should hurry toward the good
and restrain one's thoughts from the bad.
If a person is slow in doing good,
one's mind will find pleasure in wrong.

Dhammapada 116

HINDUISM

Wisdom is the boat
that would carry you across the sea of all sin.

Bhagavad Gita 4.36

As a fire is obscured by smoke . . .
so wisdom is obscured by desire.

Bhagavad Gita 3.38

JUDAISM

Turn from evil and do good.

Psalm 34.14*

Stop doing wrong, learn to do right!

Isaiah 1.16*

I have set before you life and death, blessings and curses.
Now choose life.

*Deuteronomy 30.19**

CONFUCIANISM

The sense of right and wrong
is the starting point of Wisdom.

Mencius II.A.6

TAOISM

He who knows what is of God
and who knows what is of Man
has reached indeed the height of wisdom.

Chuang Tzu 6

Right and wrong they confound . . .
Evildoers call crooked what is straight,
straight what is crooked.

Treatise on Response & Retribution, part 3

avoid wrongdoing and its
consequences.

CHRISTIANITY

The wages of sin is death.

Romans 6.23

ISLAM

Evil will recoil on those that plot evil.

Qur'an 35.43

You start the day and are vendor of your soul,
    either freeing it or bringing about its ruin.

Forty Hadith of an-Nawawi 22

BUDDHISM

Pain is the outcome of evil.

Dhammapada 117

Avoid wrongdoing, just as a merchant with a small escort
    and great wealth avoids a dangerous route,
just as one who loves life avoids poison.

Dhammapada 123

HINDUISM

It is possible to escape other enemies,
    but your own hateful acts will pursue and destroy you.
As a shadow follows footsteps wherever they go,
    even so will destruction pursue those
    who commit sinful deeds.

Tirukkural 207-208

JUDAISM

But if you do not do what is right,
    sin is crouching at your door.

Genesis 4.7*

"A sage who fears sin—to what is this sage comparable?"
"Lo, such a one is a craftsman with tools in hand."
"A sage who does not fear sin?"
"Lo, this is a craftsman without tools."

The Fathers According to Rabbi Nathan XXII.I-III

CONFUCIANISM

The inferior person thinks small sins do no harm,
    and so does not give them up.
Thus sins accumulate
    until they can no longer be covered up,
and guilt becomes so great
    that it can no longer be wiped out.

I Ching, Great Commentary 2.5.8

TAOISM

The right way leads forward; the wrong way backward.
Do not proceed on an evil path. Do not sin in secret.

Treatise on Response & Retribution, part 1

see your life as a journey—
choose a wise path.

LET YOURSELF BE LED BY YOUR HEART,

AND YOU WILL NEVER LOSE YOUR WAY.

AFRICAN TRADITIONAL RELIGIONS. *Egyptian proverb*

CHRISTIANITY

Let your eyes look straight ahead,
    fix your gaze directly before you . . .
Do not swerve to the right or the left;
    keep your foot from evil.

Proverbs 4.25, 27*

The gate is wide and the road is easy
    that leads to destruction,
    and there are many who take it.
For the gate is narrow and the road is hard that leads to life,
    and there are few who find it.

Matthew 7.13-14

ISLAM

May Allah guide you on a right path.

Qur'an 48.2

Do not wonder at the small number of those
    who follow the right path . . .
Oh people, whoever treads the clear path of guidance
    reaches the spring of water,
        and whoever abandons it strays into waterless desert.
                        Shiite. *Nahjul Balagha, sermon 200*

BUDDHISM

I see the seekers of the way growing disheartened
    in midjourney,
unable to pass over the steep road of birth and death
    and earthly desires.
Now you must press forward diligently
so that together you may reach the place where the treasure is.
                        The Lotus Sutra, chapter 7

Many beings run up and down the water's edge,
    only a few will reach the other shore.
                        Dhammapada 85

HINDUISM

He is the only Path to life eternal . . .
    He is the bridge supreme which leads to immortality.
                        Svetasvatara Upanishad 6.15, 19

When the five senses and the mind are still, and reason
    itself rests in silence, then begins the Path supreme.
                        Katha Upanishad 1.6.9

Sages say the path is narrow and difficult to tread,
    narrow as the edge of a razor.
                        Katha Upanishad 1.3.14

JUDAISM

I guide you in the way of wisdom
  and lead you along straight paths.
When you walk, your steps will not be hampered;
  when you run, you will not stumble.

Proverbs 4.11-12*

If my steps have turned from the path,
  if my heart has been led by my eyes . . .
then may others eat what I have sown
  and may my crops be uprooted.

Job 31.7-8*

CONFUCIANISM

It is difficult to escape in the present age.
  Who can go out but by the door?
How is it that people will not walk according to these ways?

Analects 6.14-15

The way of truth is like a great road.
  It is not difficult to know it.
The trouble is only that people will not seek it.

Mencius VI.B.2

TAOISM

If I had just a little bit of wisdom
I should walk the Great Path and fear only straying from it.

Tao Te Ching 53

⌐

see your heart as a garden—
plant it well.

THIS WORLD IS A GARDEN, THE LORD ITS GARDENER,

CHERISHING ALL, NONE NEGLECTED.

SIKHISM. *Guru Granth Sahib, Majh Ashtpadi, p. 118*

CHRISTIANITY

A farmer went out to sow his seed . . .
    some fell along the path . . . some fell on rock . . .
    other seed fell among thorns . . .
    still other seed fell on good soil . . .
The seed is the word of God.
The seed on good soil stands for those with a noble and
    good heart, who hear the word, retain it,
    and by persevering produce a crop.

Luke 8.5-8, 11, 15

ISLAM

Those that give away their wealth from a desire
    to please Allah and to reassure their own souls
    are like a garden on a hillside:
if a shower falls upon it,
    it yields up twice its normal produce;
and if no rain falls, it is watered by the dew.

Qur'an 2.265

Good soil yields fruit by Allah's will.

Qur'an 7.58

BUDDHISM

Those who seek the Buddha way,
    have planted many good roots,
and are firm and deeply committed in mind . . .
    constantly cultivating a compassionate mind.

Lotus Sutra, chapter 3

Like a beautiful flower, full of color and full of scent,
are the fine and fruitful words of those who act accordingly.

Dhammapada 52

HINDUISM

That one plant should be sown
    and another be produced cannot happen;
whatever seed is sown,
    a plant of that kind even comes forth.

Laws of Manu 9.40

JUDAISM

If you do away with the yoke of oppression,
  with the pointing finger and malicious talk,
and if you spend yourselves in behalf of the hungry
  and satisfy the needs of the oppressed . . .
You will be like a well-watered garden,
  like a spring whose waters never fail.

*Isaiah 58.9-11**

CONFUCIANISM

Heaven nourishes the growing sprout.

The Doctrine of the Mean 17.3

TAOISM

The heart, though spiritual and mysterious,
  yet possesses a solid, tangible soil,
  which can be watered and tilled.

Tract of the Quiet Way

Set firm in the Way, none will uproot you.

Tao Te Ching 54

⁓

see goodness as a light—turn it on.

BE AS A LAMP UNTO THEM THAT WALK IN DARKNESS,

A JOY TO THE SORROWFUL, A SEA FOR THE THIRSTY,

A HAVEN FOR THE DISTRESSED,

AN UPHOLDER AND DEFENDER OF THE VICTIM OF OPPRESSION.

BAHA'I FAITH. *Gleanings from the Writings of Bahá'u'lláh*

CHRISTIANITY

You are the light of the world.

Matthew 5.14

Whoever lives by the truth comes into the light.

John 3.21

Whoever loves a brother or sister lives in the light,
    and in such a one there is no cause for stumbling.

I John 2.10

ISLAM

Those who believe, their light will gleam before them
    and on their right hands—
they will say: Our Lord, make perfect for us our light,
    and grant us protection;
surely you are Possessor of Power over all things.

Qur'an 66.8

BUDDHISM

The holy shine even from afar,
   like distant mountain peaks covered with snow.

Dhammapada 304

The sun shines by day; the moon lights up the night;
the warriors shine in their armor;
   the holy one shines in meditation;
but the awakened shines radiantly all day and night.

Dhammapada 387

HINDUISM

When you have seen the Truth of the Spirit,
   you are one with him . . .
Then your soul becomes a lamp by which you find the
   Truth of Brahman.
This is the God whose light illumines all creation.

Svetasvatara Upanishad 2.15-16

JUDAISM

The path of the righteous is like the first gleam of dawn,
   shining ever brighter till the full light of day.

*Proverbs 4.18**

Your word is a lamp to my feet and a light for my path.

*Psalm 119.105**

A person that people like to be with is good.
A person who keeps that goodness within is genuine.
One who fully develops that goodness is called "excellent."
One whose full development of goodness shines forth is
    called "great."

Mencius VII.B.25

TAOISM

Look at this window: It is nothing but a hole in the wall,
    but because of it the whole room is full of light.
So when the faculties are empty, the heart is full of light.
Being full of light it becomes an influence
    by which others are secretly transformed.

Chuang Tzu 4

Use your own light and return to the source of light.
    This is called practicing eternity.

Tao Te Ching 52

choose your companions wisely.

CHRISTIANITY

Do not be misled: Bad company corrupts good character.

I Corinthians 15.33

He who walks with the wise grows wise,
   but a companion of fools suffers harm.

*Proverbs 13.20**

ISLAM

Avoid those that treat their faith as a sport and a pastime
   and are seduced by the life of this world.

Qur'an 6.70

BUDDHISM

As the person you make your friend,
   as the one you follow, such do you yourself become.

Itivuttaka 68-69

He who walks in the company of fools suffers a long way.

Dhammapada 207

HINDUISM

As water changes according to the soil
    through which it flows,
so do you assimilate the character of your associates.

Tirukkural 452

Wisdom, appearing to originate in one's mind,
    has its source in one's companions.

Tirukkural 454

The wise befriend the wise and keep that friendship constant.

Tirukkural 425

JUDAISM

What is attached to the defiled will be defiled;
    and what is attached to the pure will be pure.

Kelim 12.2

Happy are those who do not follow the advice of the wicked,
    or take the path that sinners tread,
    or sit in the seat of scoffers.

Psalm 1.1-2*

CONFUCIANISM

Make faithfulness and truth your masters:
    have no friends unlike yourself.

Analects 9.25

In making friends, befriend a person's Integrity.

Mencius V.B.3

Those that are good, seek for friends;
    that will help you to practice virtue with body and soul.
Those that are wicked, keep at a distance;
    it will prevent evil from approaching you.

Tract of the Quiet Way

learn from a wise mentor.

WHEN THE WISDOMKEEPERS SPEAK, ALL SHOULD LISTEN.

NATIVE AMERICAN RELIGIONS. *Seneca proverb*

CHRISTIANITY

Imitate those who through faith and patience inherit
   what has been promised.

Hebrews 6.12

Let one who is righteous rebuke me—it is oil on my head.
   My head will not refuse it.

Psalm 141.5*

Hold onto instruction, do not let it go; guard it well,
   for it is your life.

Proverbs 4.13*

ISLAM

The learned ones . . . leave knowledge as their inheritance:
   Those who inherit it inherit a great fortune.

Hadith of Bukhari

BUDDHISM

If you see an intelligent person who tells you where true
    treasures are to be found,
who shows what is to be avoided, and administers
    reproofs,
follow that wise person.

Dhammapada 76

HINDUISM

The most precious wealth is the wealth acquired by the ear.
Indeed, of all wealth that wealth is paramount . . .
Words from the lips of the upright
    are like a steadying staff in a slippery place.

Tirukkural 411, 415

JUDAISM

Let your house be a gathering place for the wise;
be covered by the dust of their feet,
    and drink in their words with thirst . . .
Choose yourself a mentor.

Abot 1.4, 6

CONFUCIANISM

A skillful teacher leads and does not drag,
    strengthens and does not discourage.
Leading and not dragging produces harmony.
Strengthening and not discouraging makes attainment easy.

Book of Rites 16.13

Find a teacher who is an integral being,
a beacon who extends her light and virtue with equal ease
to those who appreciate her and those who don't.
Shape yourself in her mold, bathe in her nourishing radiance,
and reflect it out to the rest of the world.

Hua Hu Ching 75

think for yourself.

A FOOL AND WATER WILL GO THE WAY THEY ARE DIVERTED.

AFRICAN TRADITIONAL RELIGIONS.

Ethiopian proverb

CHRISTIANITY

Test everything. Hold fast to what is good.

I Thessalonians 5.21

In regard to evil be infants, but in your thinking be adults.

I Corinthians 14.20

ISLAM

Do not accept any information,
    unless you verify it for yourself.
I have given you the hearing, the eyesight, and the brain,
    and you are responsible for using them.

Qur'an 17.36

BUDDHISM

Do not believe in anything
    simply because you have heard it . . .
Do not believe in anything
    simply because it is found written in your religious books.

Do not believe in anything
    merely on the authority of your teachers and elders.
But when, after observation and analysis,
    you find anything that agrees with reason,
and is conducive to the good and benefit of one and all,
    then accept it and live up to it.

Anguttara-nikaya, Kalama Sutra

HINDUISM

Without investigation, trust no one.

Tirukkural 509

The deeper a sandwell is dug the more freely its water flows.
Even so, the deeper one's learning,
    the greater is one's wisdom.

Tirukkural 396

JUDAISM

The simple believe everything,
    but the prudent give thought to their steps.

Proverbs 14.15*

CONFUCIANISM

To learn and never think—that's delusion.

Analects 2.15

Learning extensively, and having a firm and sincere aim;
inquiring with earnestness,
    and reflecting with self-application:
virtue is in such a course.

Analects 19.6

TAOISM

Rather than base one's judgment
on the opinions of the many,
let each look after his own affairs.

Chuang Tzu 11

labyrinth walking

the labyrinth can be traced back through 4,000 years of history, and its design is found in almost every major religious tradition in the world.

Native American Hopis called it the "Mother Earth symbol." The Crusaders used the labyrinth to symbolically represent the pilgrimage to the Holy Land. Today, among other reasons, we enter the labyrinth to find our sacred inner space—our center.

The labyrinth is a metaphor of our spiritual life. It is a meandering yet purposeful path, representing a journey to our own center and back again out into the world.

A labyrinth is not a maze. The tortuous path of a maze is filled with forks, dead-ends and blind alleys; in contrast, a labyrinth offers only one route. Navigating a maze requires our analytical, problem-solving left brain; while focusing on the process of moving through the labyrinth allows us to shift into a harmonious, receptive state, where we can receive spiritual guidance.

No matter where we stand in the twists and turns of the labyrinth's circuits, we can always see the center. Once we take our first step, the path itself gently and faultlessly leads us to the center of both the labyrinth and ourselves. While a maze is full of choices, a labyrinth presents only one: whether or not to enter the path.

Most popular today are the seven-circuit design, seen above, and the twelve-circuit design (or eleven-circuit, if you don't count the center), seen to the left. The Roman design is illustrated below. Labyrinths range from finger-walking screensaver size to a group-accommodating 80-foot width. Their paths are often cut into turf, laid out with stones, or painted on the ground.

Here are some labyrinth-walking guidelines:

FOCUS. Be quiet and still at the entrance for a few moments. If you are seeking spiritual guidance, focus on your question.

ENTER. Walk purposefully at your own pace. Observe the process.

PAUSE. When you reach the center, stay there —physically and mentally—as long as you desire, quiet and receptive. If you entered with a question, ask it here, in a meditative manner.

REFLECT. When you feel ready, retrace your steps outward. Use the return journey to reflect on your experience.

The labyrinth is a tool for people of all beliefs to come together in a common spiritual experience. The experience will vary from person to person, from pleasant to profound. Each time is different. You may hear Spirit speak in a very simple and quiet way; you may recognize the patterns of life that are healthy or not so helpful. You may even be challenged to reshape your life.

7

from a heart of discipline

i have been lucky enough to sit at the deathbed of three people whose spiritual greatness I was certain of: my great friend, Anne Pennington, a professor of Slavic languages; a Tibetan adept, Thuksey Rinpoche, whom I met in Ladakh in 1980; and the man whom I revere as my soul's father, Fr. Bede Griffiths. In each case, I was amazed by the depth of discipline that death uncovered and the depth of commitment to prayer.

While Anne lay dying, she kept repeating the words of the Lord's prayer in Church Slavonic. Thuksey Rinpoche never ceased to tell his rosary and repeat "Om mani Padme pani hum," and even when Father Bede was extremely weak with pain, he found the strength to say the Jesus prayer or the Hail Mary.

What I immediately understood was that such a commitment to discipline had nothing to do with fear of death.
None of these three beings was afraid of the world they were
going into; they were all profound mystics whose minds and
hearts had been irradiated by divine light and who knew
their own immortality and the certainty of God's mercy.
Why they were praying, I saw, was because they wanted at all
moments to be in the stream of remembrance of God and so
bathed in the illumination of their own true nature. What
they were afraid of was not death itself but of not meeting
death with as full and radiant a consciousness as possible,
with their whole being offered up in gratitude, sacred passion, and adoration.

I realized too that the discipline I was witnessing had
always been a secret force within them. I had loved each of
them for their tremendous kindness, sweetness, clarity, and
strength, and for an indefinable atmosphere of simple holi-
ness that accompanied them. Now, as they lay dying, I understood that these qualities were not only divine graces and
gifts, but they were also the reward of a lifetime of secret
passion for the Divine, a lifetime of incessant discipline of
self-analysis, spiritual practice, and abandonment to adoration and praise.

The last time I saw Fr. Bede, I asked for his blessing and
one final word of advice.

He held my face in his hands and then said, "Pray, pray
always!"

And he went back to his prayers.

Andrew Harvey

acknowledge your inner conflict.

I SEEK STRENGTH, NOT TO BE GREATER THAN MY BROTHER,

BUT TO FIGHT MY GREATEST ENEMY—MYSELF.

NATIVE AMERICAN RELIGIONS. *Chief Yellow Lark, Lakota*

CHRISTIANITY

The spirit indeed is willing, but the flesh is weak.

Matthew 26.41

When I want to do good, evil is right there with me.
For in my inner being I delight in God's law;
but I see another law at work in the members of my body,
    waging war against the law of my mind.

Romans 7.21-23

ISLAM

I do not declare myself free;
most surely one's self has a habit
    of commanding one to do evil.

Qur'an 12.53

O Allah! I seek refuge in you from impure deeds
    and evil habits.

Hadith of Bukhari

BUDDHISM

How have I been used like a slave
    by enemies such as hatred and craving?
For while they dwell within my mind,
    at their pleasure they cause me harm,
yet I patiently endure them without any anger;
      but this is an inappropriate
      and shameful time for patience . . .
How can I be joyful and unafraid
    if in my heart I readily prepare a place
for this incessant enemy of long duration?

Shantideva, Guide to the Bodhisattva's Way of Life 4.28-35

HINDUISM

What is the force that binds us to selfish deeds, O Krishna?
What power moves us, even against our will,
    as if forcing us?
It is selfish desire and anger . . .
Selfish desire is found in the senses, mind, and intellect,
    misleading them and burying wisdom in delusion.
Fight with all your strength, Arjuna!

Bhagavad Gita 3.36-41

JUDAISM

We desire to do your will. And what prevents us?
That bacteria—the evil inclination—which infects us.
It is obvious to you that
    we do not have the strength to resist it . . .
Vanquish it from before us, and subdue it,

so that we may do your will as our own will,
  with a whole heart.

Jersusalem Talmud, Berakhot 4.2

CONFUCIANISM

When Heaven sends down calamities,
  there is hope of weathering them;
when people bring them upon themselves,
  there is no hope of escape.

Mencius IV.A.8

TAOISM

Desires wither the heart.

Tao Te Ching 12

control your thoughts.

WHOEVER OWNS THE INNER SQUARE OF THE HOUSE

IS THE MASTER OF THE OUTER.

AFRICAN TRADITIONAL RELIGIONS. *Yoruba proverb*

CHRISTIANITY

Whatever is true, whatever is noble,
    whatever is right, whatever is pure,
whatever is lovely, whatever is admirable—
if anything is excellent or praiseworthy—
    think about such things.

Philippians 4.8

We do not wage war as the world does . . .
We take captive every thought to make it obedient to Christ.

II Corinthians 10.4-5

ISLAM

O Lord my God, in you I take refuge . . .
from the evil one who lies in wait
    only to whisper temptations into our minds
    and then withdraws,
who suggests evil thoughts in our hearts.

Qur'an 114.1-5

BUDDHISM

Just like one would quickly, fearfully
pick up a dropped sword,
so one should pick up the dropped sword
of mindfulness . . .
Just as a poison spreads throughout the body
once it has reached the blood,
so does a fault spread throughout the mind
once it has reached a vulnerable spot.

A Guide to the Bodhisattva Way of Life 7.67-79

Whatever an enemy might do . . .
the ill-directed mind can do to you even worse.

Dhammapada 42

HINDUISM

The chariot of the mind is drawn by wild horses,
and those wild horses have to be tamed.

Svetasvatara Upanishad 2.9

However often the restless mind may break loose and wander,
you should rein it in and constantly bring it back.

Bhagavad Gita 6.26

Serenity, gentleness . . . purity of being, compassion—
this is control of the mind.

Bhagavad Gita 17.16

JUDAISM

Those of steadfast mind you keep in peace—
in peace because they trust in you.

*Isaiah 26.3**

Deep in the illuminated mind is no storm.

The Odes of Solomon 34

CONFUCIANISM

The cultivation of the person
    lies in the correction of the mind.
When you are angry, you cannot be correct.
When you are frightened, you cannot be correct;
when there is something you desire, you cannot be correct;
when there is something you are anxious about,
    you cannot be correct.

The Great Learning, chapter 7

TAOISM

If there is not inner repose,
your mind will be galloping about
    though you are sitting still.

Chuang Tzu 4

If you close your mind in judgments
    and traffic with desires,
your heart will be troubled.
If you keep your mind from judging
    and aren't led by the senses,
your heart will find peace.

Tao Te Ching 52

meditate.

MORTALS, FORESTS, BLADES OF GRASS, ANIMALS AND BIRDS

ALL MEDITATE ON YOU.

SIKHISM. *Guru Granth Sahib, Asa Chhant, p. 455*

CHRISTIANITY

We meditate on your unfailing love.

Psalm 48.9*

Oh, how I love your law! I meditate on it all day long.

Psalm 119.97*

When you are on your beds,
　　search your hearts and be silent.

Psalm 4.4*

ISLAM

In the privacy of the night
　　the worshipers of the Most Gracious
meditate on their Lord, and fall prostrate.

Qur'an 25.64

BUDDHISM

While in the same way that rain
    cannot break into a well-roofed house,
desire cannot break into a mind
    that has been practicing meditation well.

Dhammapada 14

HINDUISM

Concentrating the mind on a single object,
    controlling the thoughts
    and the activities of the senses,
let the yogi practice meditation for self-purification.

Bhagavad Gita 6.12

Resolve to become a person of meditation.
The person of meditation is considered by me
    as the most devoted
who, with heart fixed on me, full of faith, worships me.

Bhagavad Gita 6.47

JUDAISM

My eyes stay open through the watches of the night,
    that I may meditate on your promises.

Psalm 119.148*

Do not let this book of the Law depart from your mouth;
    meditate on it day and night,
so that you may be careful to do everything written in it.

Joshua 1.8*

CONFUCIANISM

For you to give full realization to your mind or heart
    is for you to understand your own nature,
and when you know your own nature,
    you will know Heaven.
By retaining your mind or heart and nurturing your nature
    you are serving Heaven.

Mencius VII.A.1

TAOISM

In meditation, go deep in the heart.

Tao Te Ching 8

If you can empty your mind of all thoughts
    your heart will embrace the tranquility of peace . . .
Returning to the source is tranquility.

Tao Te Ching 16

control your words.

IT DOES NOT REQUIRE MANY WORDS TO SPEAK THE TRUTH.
NATIVE AMERICAN RELIGIONS. *Chief Joseph, Nez Perce*

CHRISTIANITY

Those who consider themselves religious
    but do not keep a tight rein on their tongues,
they deceive themselves and their religion is worthless.

James 1.26

The mouths of the wise are guided by their hearts.

Proverbs 16.23*

ISLAM

Whoever believes in Allah and the Last Day
    should either speak good, or better remain silent.

Hadith of Muslim

Whoever guarantees me the chastity of what is between
    the legs, and what is between the jaws,
to them I guarantee Paradise.

Hadith of Bukhari

BUDDHISM

Better than a thousand meaningless words
is one word of deep meaning, which when heard, brings peace.

Dhammapada 100

Speak only endearing speech, speech that is welcomed.
Speech when it brings no evil to others is pleasant.

Sutta Nipata 454

HINDUISM

To utter harsh words when sweet ones would serve
is like eating unripe fruits when ripe ones are at hand.

Tirukkural 100

You may neglect everything else,
   but be ever vigilant in restraining your tongue.
Those who fail to do so meet with great trouble.

Tirukkural 127

JUDAISM

I will watch my ways and keep my tongue from sin;
   I will put a muzzle on my mouth.

Psalm 39.1*

Said the Holy One, blessed be he, to the tongue . . .
I have set up as protection for you two walls,
one of bone (the teeth) and one of flesh (the cheeks).

Arakhin 15b-16a

When words are many, sin is not absent;
   but the prudent are restrained in speech.

Proverbs 10.19*

CONFUCIANISM

Listen much, keep silent when in doubt,
    and always take heed of the tongue;
you will make few mistakes.

Analects 2.18

TAOISM

Those who know do not talk. Those who talk do not know.

Tao Te Ching 56

The more you talk, the more nonsense you utter. . .
You wag your lips and make your tongue a drumstick.

The Writings of Chuang Tzu, book XXIX.III.VII.1

be aware of the power of your tongue.

A CUTTING WORD IS WORSE THAN A BOWSTRING;

A CUT MAY HEAL, BUT THE CUT OF THE TONGUE DOES NOT.

AFRICAN TRADITIONAL RELIGIONS. *Mauritania proverb*

~

CHRISTIANITY

The tongue has the power of life and death.

Proverbs 18.21*

Consider what a great forest is set on fire by a small spark.
The tongue also is a fire . . .
    It sets the whole course of a person's life on fire.

James 3.5-6

ISLAM

Is there anything that topples people on their faces into
    hellfire other than the harvests of their tongues?

Forty Hadith of an-Nawawi 29

Tongue is a beast; if it is let loose, it devours.

Shiite. *Nahjul Balagha, saying 60*

BUDDHISM

People are born with an axe in their mouths,
and they cut themselves with it
    when they speak foolish words.

Sutta Nipata 657

HINDUISM

The goodness of all your virtues can be lost
    by speaking even a single word of injury.
The wound caused by fire heals in its time;
    the burn inflicted by an inflamed tongue never heals.

Tirukkural 128-129

JUDAISM

Just as the hand can commit murder,
    so the tongue can commit murder . . .
Scripture states, "Their tongue is a sharpened arrow"
    (Jer. 9.7).
It can commit murder even from a distance like an arrow.

Arakhin 15b-16a

The tongue that brings healing is a tree of life,
    but a deceitful tongue crushes the spirit.

Proverbs 15.4*

CONFUCIANISM

I hate a sharp tongue, the ruin of kingdom and home.

Analects 17.18

The petty words which they speak are poison to a person.

Chuang Tzu 32

control yourself.

DIFFICULT TO CONQUER IS ONESELF;

BUT WHEN THAT IS CONQUERED, EVERYTHING IS CONQUERED.

JAINISM. *Uttaradhyayana Sutra 9.34-36*

CHRISTIANITY

Train yourself in godliness,
for while physical training is of some value,
    godliness is valuable in every way.

I Timothy 4.7-8

The fruit of the Spirit is love, joy, peace, patience,
    kindness, goodness, faithfulness,
    gentleness, and self-control.

Galatians 5.22-23

ISLAM

Guard yourselves against temptation.

Qur'an 8.25

The strong are not the ones
    who overcome the people by strength,
but the strong are the ones
    who control themselves while in anger.

Hadith of Bukhari

BUDDHISM

Control yourself, as a merchant controls a spirited horse.

Dhammapada 380

Irrigators lead the waters; fletchers bend the shafts;
carpenters bend the wood; the wise control themselves.

Dhammapada 80

HINDUISM

Guard your self-control as a precious treasure,
    for there is no greater wealth in life than this.

Tirukkural 122

JUDAISM

Like a city whose walls are broken down
    is one who lacks self-control.

Proverbs 25.28*

One who is slow to anger is better than the mighty,
and one whose temper is controlled
    than one who captures a city.

Proverbs 16.32*

CONFUCIANISM

Keep a firm grasp on your will.

Mencius II.A.2

If you can one day renovate yourself, do so from day to day.
    Yea, let there be daily renovation.

The Great Learning, Commentary

The one who conquers others has physical strength;
The one who conquers one's self is strong.

Tao Te Ching 33

In caring for others and serving heaven,
     there is nothing like using restraint.
Restraint begins with giving up one's own ideas.

Tao Te Ching 59

guard against lust.

THE HERO DOES NOT TOLERATE DISCONTENT.

THE HERO DOES NOT TOLERATE LUST.

BECAUSE THE HERO IS NOT CARELESS . . .

THOSE WHOM LUST CONQUERS, SINK;

THEREFORE DO NOT SHRINK FROM THE HARD CONTROL.

JAINISM. *Acaranga Sutra 2.6.3; 6.5.5*

CHRISTIANITY

Abstain from fleshly lusts, which war against the soul.

I Peter 2.11

One is tempted by one's own desire,
    being lured and enticed by it;
then, when that desire has conceived, it gives birth to sin,
and that sin, when it is fully grown, gives birth to death.

James 1.14-15

ISLAM

Do you know what most commonly brings people
    into hell?
It is the two hollow things: the mouth and the private parts.

Hadith of Tirmidhi

The best of you are those
who have the most excellent morals.

Hadith of Bukhari

BUDDHISM

Not by a shower of gold coins
does contentment arise in sensual pleasures.

Dhammapada 186

HINDUISM

Desire never rests by enjoyment of lusts,
as fire surely increases the more butter is offered to it.

Laws of Manu 2.94

JUDAISM

Jealousy, lust, and ambition drive a person
out of this world.

Abot 4.22

Remember all the commands of the Lord,
that you may obey them
and not prostitute yourselves
by going after the lusts of your own hearts and eyes.

Numbers 15.40*

I made a covenant with my eyes
not to look lustfully at a girl.

Job 31.1*

CONFUCIANISM

The superior man is on guard against three things:
When he is a young man and his physical energies
    are not yet settled,
    he is on guard against lust.
When he is mature and his physical energy is solid,
    he is on guard against being drawn into a fight.
When he is old, and his physical power is weakened,
    he is on guard not to cling to his attainments.

Analects 16.7

TAOISM

The cords of passion and desire
    weave a binding net around you.

Hua Hu Ching 70

Those who are bound by desire see only the outward container.

Tao Te Ching 1

conquer vices.

CHRISTIANITY

Do not get drunk on wine, which leads to debauchery.
    Instead, be filled with the Spirit.

Ephesians 5.18

Everything is permissible for me—
    but not everything is beneficial.
Everything is permissible for me—
    but I will not be mastered by anything.

I Corinthians 6.12

ISLAM

Wine and games of chance . . .
    are abominations devised by Satan.
Avoid them, so that you may prosper.
Satan seeks to stir up enmity and hatred among you
    by means of wine and gambling.

Qur'an 5.90

BUDDHISM

Encircled with craving, people hop around and around
   like a rabbit caught in a snare.

Dhammapada 342

Just as a tree, though cut down, sprouts up again
   if its roots remain uncut and firm, even so,
   until the craving that lies dormant is rooted out,
suffering springs up again and again.

Dhammapada 338

HINDUISM

Those who constantly drink are like ones who take poison.

Tirukkural 926

Do not take to gambling even if you can win,
for your wins will be like the baited hooks that fish swallow.

Tirukkural 931

JUDAISM

Woe to those who rise early in the morning
   to run after their drinks,
who stay up late at night till they are inflamed with wine.

Isaiah 5.11*

CONFUCIANISM

Do not be a servant to wine.

Analects 9.15

A choice of meats could not tempt Confucius to eat more . . .
he did not drink till he got fuddled.

Analects 10.8

TAOISM

Glutting with food and drink,
hoarding wealth and possessions—
these are the ways of theft, and far from the Way.

Tao Te Ching 53

~

exercise moderation.

THERE ARE THREE THINGS THAT IF PEOPLE DO NOT KNOW,

THEY CANNOT LIVE LONG IN THIS WORLD:

WHAT IS TOO MUCH FOR THEM,

WHAT IS TOO LITTLE FOR THEM

AND WHAT IS JUST RIGHT FOR THEM.

AFRICAN TRADITIONAL RELIGIONS. *Swahili proverb*

CHRISTIANITY

Do not wear yourself out to get rich;
    have the wisdom to show restraint.
Do not join those who drink too much wine
    or gorge themselves on meat,
for drunkards and gluttons become poor.
Buy the truth and do not sell it;
    get wisdom, discipline and understanding.

Proverbs 23.4, 20-21, 23*

ISLAM

Lord, forgive us our sins and our excesses.

Qur'an 3.147

Be moderate and stand firm in trouble.

Hadith of Muslim

BUDDHISM

Look at the undisciplined, those who are intemperate.
Take care lest desire and worldliness
   introduce you to long suffering.

Dhammapada 248

Be moderate in eating.

Dhammapada 185

HINDUISM

Call that the "true piety"
   which most removes Earthaches and ills,
where one is moderate in eating and in resting, and in
      sport;
measured in wish and act.

Bhagavad Gita 6.17-18

JUDAISM

Do not be overrighteous, neither be overwise—
   why destroy yourself?
The person who fears God will avoid all extremes.

Ecclesiastes 7.16,18*

CONFUCIANISM

Only when one will not do some things,
   is one capable of doing great things.

Mencius IV.B.8

Confucius was not a man of extremes.

Mencius IV.B.10

TAOISM

Out of compassion the wise avoid extravagance,
   excess, and the extremes.

Tao Te Ching 29

Fill a cup to its brim and it is easily spilled;
temper a sword to its sharpest and it is easily broken . . .

Tao Te Ching 9

One must know when to stop.
   Knowing when to stop averts trouble.

Tao Te Ching 32

persevere through adversity.

A LIMP FORWARD IS A GAIN IN DISTANCE.

AFRICAN TRADITIONAL RELIGIONS. *Gbagyi proverb*

CHRISTIANITY

Blessed are those who persevere under trial.
They have stood the test and will receive the crown of life.

James 1.12

We rejoice in our sufferings, because we know that suffering produces perseverance; perseverance, character;
and character, hope.

Romans 5.3-4

ISLAM

Surely within every crisis, there is opportunity.
Yes, within every crisis, there is opportunity.
So when you are at your end, let the Lord fill your mind,
strengthen your heart,
and allow his grace to restore your soul.

Qur'an 94.5-8

Good news to those who endure with fortitude . . .
such people are rightly guided.

Qur'an 2.156-157

BUDDHISM

Good people walk on, whatever befalls them.

Dhammapada 83

HINDUISM

In the midst of cold and heat, pleasure and pain,
    as well as honor and dishonor,
the person who is unmoved,
whose senses are restrained . . .
    is said to be spiritually disciplined.

Bhagavad Gita 6.7-8

JUDAISM

Though the righteous fall seven times, they rise again.

Proverbs 24.16*

Be strong and do not give up, for your work will be rewarded.

II Chronicles 15.7*

When God has tested me, I will come forth as gold.

Job 23.10*

CONFUCIANISM

Integrity, wisdom, skill, intelligence—
    such things are forged in adversity.

Mencius VII.A.18

TAOISM

The gentlest thing in the world
    overcomes the hardest thing in the world.

Tao Te Ching 43

fasting

it would be difficult to name any major tradition that does not value the benefits of fasting, in one form or another. Fasting is a spiritual discipline practiced by virtually every religion.

At its roots, fasting means to abstain from food either partially or completely for a set period of time. By extension, "fasting of the heart" is to refrain from any number of worldly indulgences.

Some religions impose specific times and rules for fasting. Islam's month of Ramadan, Hinduism's Thaipusam Festival, and Judaism's Yom Kippur fall into this group. Christianity promotes fasting for specific, individual purposes and leaves the methodology up to the believer. Other traditions, including Buddhism, Taoism, and Confucianism, encourage a fasting of the heart—not only a daily moderation in eating (vegetarianism, for example), but a continuous detaching from all senses.

Certainly, disparity abounds. But if we dig beneath these variations in the outer forms of fasting, some deeper common goals emerge:

1. Self-Control. The more we indulge our senses, the greater become their demands. Fasting tells our senses, in no uncertain terms, that they are not in charge. And our willingness to yield to Spirit is dependent on our will not being ruled by our senses. Simply put, fasting denies our physical senses for the sake of spiritual growth.

2. Purification. The connection between body, mind, and spirit is undeniable. What occurs at one level is reflected at the other levels. When we cleanse our bodies through fasting, a parallel course of cleansing our thoughts and hearts comes more easily.

3. Compassion. The very real pangs of hunger that we experience after missing a couple of meals awaken our sympathy for what the poor and destitute feel everyday.

4. Dependency. We often cling to a facade of independence and self-sufficiency. It's easy to believe such notions on a full belly, but raw hunger shakes up our perceptions and reminds us of our human frailty. Our mortality in turn reminds us of our dependence on Spirit for things far more important than food.

GUIDELINES FOR FASTING

1. Focus on a meaningful purpose for your fast.

2. Determine ahead of time how long you will fast. It might be one meal or one day or three days; you might choose to skip one meal each day for a week. The variations are unlimited.

3. Choose what you will give up. All food? Meat? Sweets? Salt? What about smoking? Caffeine? Negative and immoral thoughts? How about television? The idea is to sacrifice something that will cost you. A word of warning: If you are susceptible to eating disorders, or if you

are pregnant, nursing, elderly, or frail, avoid fasting from food. It could be dangerous to your health.

4. During the fast, channel your thoughts and actions toward your selected purpose. If you are fasting for the sake of compassion, take the money you would've spent on food and give it to the poor. If you are fasting from television in order to draw closer to Spirit, you could spend your time praying and reading scriptures.

5. Be aware that the first day is usually the most difficult. At this point you will probably encounter a battle of the will. Stick with it! This is where you take control of your senses. The spiritual breakthrough you gain will be well worth the war.

8

from a heart of surrender

meister Eckhart wrote, "A perfect and true will is one that is always totally aligned with God and empty of everything else. The more a person succeeds in following God's will, the more he or she unites his depth with God's. By aligning with God's will, a person takes on the taste of God. Grief and joy, bitterness and sweetness, darkness and light, and all of life become a divine gift."

I have kept this quote on a stand on my desk for twenty years to remind me of the secret to unity with God—surrender to the Divine will. For me, surrendering to what God wants and demands has always been the most difficult of things. "Even Jesus," an old Kabbalist friend once reassured me, "came to surrender 'kicking and screaming' and weeping tears of blood." I never trust those who say they always find God's will easy to read or give in to. They must be either lying or mad, or one of those who, as Nietzsche put it, "imagine the real suffering is losing at cards or missing an opera they would enjoy."

I have also found that it is frequently easier to surrender to what God demands of oneself than to what God seems to ask of others, especially if they are close to you and their suffering continues without relief or meaning. Surrendering to the mystery of pain in the ones you love takes the greatest possible trust and has been for me the ultimate test of my faith.

Yet when I can surrender to what God demands of me, I find myself birthed into a boundless peaceful strength in which all things that happen—even great suffering—"taste of God," in Eckhart's marvelous words. And as I grow older and seem to find this surrender a little easier—because now experience has taught me its strange sweetness—I become almost grateful for the opportunity to give up my human reason and demands. I have learned that each surrender to God is a little death, preparing me for that great and final death into love that brings total awakening and the experience of what St. John of the Cross calls "the tenderness of the life of God."

Andrew Harvey

accept circumstances.

GOD GRANT ME THE SERENITY

TO ACCEPT THE THINGS I CANNOT CHANGE,

COURAGE TO CHANGE THE THINGS I CAN,

AND WISDOM TO KNOW THE DIFFERENCE.

TWELVE-STEP ORGANIZATIONS.

Based on "Serenity Prayer" by Reinhold Niebuhr

CHRISTIANITY

Should we accept good from God, and not trouble?

Job 2.10*

Naked I came from my mother's womb,
    and naked I will depart.
The Lord gave and the Lord has taken away;
    may the name of the Lord be praised.

Job 1.21*

Do everything without complaining or arguing.

Philippians 2.14

ISLAM

Those who surrender themselves to Allah
    and do good to others,
They indeed have taken hold of the firmest thing
    upon which one can lay hold.

Qur'an 31.22

BUDDHISM

Whether touched by pleasure or pain,
    the wise show no change of temper.

Dhammapada 83

HINDUISM

Happiness and misery, prosperity and adversity,
    gain and loss, death and life,
    in their turn, wait upon all creatures.
For this reason, the wise person of tranquil self
would be neither elated with joy nor depressed with sorrow.

Mahabharata, Santiparva 25.30-31

If you surrender your human will,
    you leave sorrows behind...

Katha Upanishad 1.2.20

JUDAISM

One should always be as soft as a reed
    and not as tough as cedar.
In the case of a reed, all the winds in the world
    can go on blowing against it but it sways with them,
so that when the winds grow silent,

[204]

it reverts and stands in place.
But in the case of a cedar it will not stand in place,
but when the south wind blows against it,
    it uproots the cedar and turns it over.

The Fathers According to Rabbi Nathan XLI.III.1

CONFUCIANISM

The noble-minded act accepting their own situation.
    They do not hope to be somewhere else.

Doctrine of the Mean 14.1.1

TAOISM

To know what you can't do anything about,
    and to be content with it as you would with fate—
only a person of virtue can do that.

Chuang Tzu 5

A tree that is unbending is easily broken.
The hard and strong will fall.
    The soft and yielding will overcome.

Tao Te Ching 76

don't let anger take over.

THE FLY CANNOT BE DRIVEN AWAY BY GETTING ANGRY AT IT.

AFRICAN TRADITIONAL RELIGIONS. *Idoma proverb (Nigeria)*

CHRISTIANITY

What causes fights and quarrels among you?
Don't they come from your desires that battle within you?

James 4.1

In your anger do not sin.
Do not let the sun go down while you are still angry.

Ephesians 4.26

ISLAM

When one of you becomes angry while standing,
you should sit down.
If the anger leaves you, well and good;
otherwise you should lie down.

Hadith of Abu Dawud

BUDDHISM

The one who controls rising anger,
    as a driver controls a racing chariot,
that one I call a true charioteer.
    Others merely hold the reins.

Dhammapada 222

Beware of bodily anger, and control your body! . . .
Beware of the anger of the tongue,
    and control your tongue! . . .
Beware of the anger of the mind, and control your mind!

Dhammapada 231-233

HINDUISM

Can there be any greater enemy to people than anger,
    which kills laughter and joy?
Of what value is anything that destroys joy?

Tirukkural 304

If you know how to control the rising anger in your mind
    and guard yourself against losing your temper,
all other virtues will seek you out.

Tirukkural 309

JUDAISM

In your anger do not sin.

Psalm 4.4*

A fool gives full vent to anger,
    but the wise quietly hold it back.

Proverbs 29.11*

Patience is better than pride.
Do not be quickly provoked in your spirit,
    for anger resides in the lap of fools.

Ecclesiastes 7.8-9*

When anger rises, think of the consequences.

Analects 16.10

Those who wish to embody the Tao
    should embrace all things.
To embrace all things means first that one holds no anger
    or resistance toward any idea or thing,
    living or dead, formed or formless.

Hua Hu Ching 3

give up natural reactions for spiritual benefits.

SUBVERT ANGER BY FORGIVENESS, SUBDUE PRIDE BY MODESTY,

OVERCOME HYPOCRISY WITH SIMPLICITY,

AND GREED BY CONTENTMENT.

JAINISM. *Samanasuttam 136*

CHRISTIANITY

All who exalt themselves will be humbled,
    and all who humble themselves will be exalted.

Matthew 23.12

Those who love their life lose it,
and those who hate their life in this world
    will keep it for eternal life.

John 12.25

ISLAM

Charity does not in any way decrease the wealth . . .
    and the one who shows humility, Allah elevates.

Hadith of Muslim

BUDDHISM

Conquer anger with love.
Conquer evil with good.
Conquer the miser with generosity
and conquer the liar with truth.

Dhammapada 223

HINDUISM

The sage awakes to light in the night of all creatures.
That which the world calls day
    is the night of ignorance to the wise.

Bhagavad Gita 2.69

JUDAISM

Those who humble themselves, the Holy One raises up;
    those who exalt themselves, the Holy One humbles.

Erubin 13b

When from a coma Rabbi Joseph recovered,
    his father asked him, "What did you see?"
He replied, "I beheld a world the reverse of this one;
    those who are on top here
    were below there, and vice versa."
He said to him, "My son,
    you have seen a corrected world."

Pesahim 50a

CONFUCIANISM

The noble-minded act in a way such that
    they conceal themselves,
    yet every day gain in luminosity.
Inferior people show themselves and every day lose luminosity.

Doctrine of the Mean 33.6

TAOISM

Yield and overcome;
    bend and be straight.
Empty out and be full;
    wear out and be renewed.
Have little and gain;
    have much and be confused.

Tao Te Ching 22

be content.

CHRISTIANITY

Godliness with contentment is great gain.
For we brought nothing into the world,
   and we can take nothing out of it.
But if we have food and clothing,
   we will be content with that.

I Timothy 6.6-8

Keep your lives free from the love of money
   and be content with what you have.

Hebrews 13.5

ISLAM

In the remembrance of Allah do hearts find satisfaction.

Qur'an 13.28

They are successful who . . . have been made contented
   by Allah with what he has given them.

Hadith of Muslim

BUDDHISM

Health is the most precious gain,
   and contentment the greatest wealth.

Dhammapada 204

HINDUISM

Contentment leads to victory of the spirit.

Tirukkural 180

There is no greater wealth than the possession of a mind
   that is free from envy.
The envying of others' possessions is equivalent to poverty.

Tirukkural 162-163

JUDAISM

A heart at peace gives life to the body,
   but envy rots the bones.

Proverbs 14.30*

I have stilled and quieted my soul;
like a weaned child with its mother,
   like a weaned child is my soul within me.

Psalm 131.2*

Who are called rich?
   Those who are content with their own portion.

Tamid 32a

CONFUCIANISM

The noble-minded do not murmur against Heaven,
    nor grumble against people.
Thus it is that the noble-minded are quiet and calm,
    waiting for the appointments of Heaven,
while the inferior person walks in dangerous paths,
    looking for lucky occurrences.

Doctrine of the Mean 14.3-4

The noble-minded are content without a full belly
    or the comforts of home.

Analects 1.14

TAOISM

Those who know they have enough are truly wealthy.

Tao Te Ching 33

Those who are contented are not disappointed.

Tao Te Ching 44

The man of perfect virtue . . .
is happy under prosperous and adverse circumstances alike.

Chuang Tzu 11

give up self-gratification to obtain true happiness.

IF ONLY THE MIND IS PURIFIED COMPLETELY,

THERE WILL BE NOTHING BUT DELIGHT IN EVERYTHING.

TENRIKYO. *Ofudesaki XIV.50*

CHRISTIANITY

The kingdom of heaven is like treasure hidden in a field.
When someone found it, he hid it again,
and then in his joy went and sold all he had
   and bought that field.

Matthew 13.44

If you keep my commandments, you will abide in my love . . .
I have told you this so that my joy may be in you,
   and that your joy may be complete.

John 15.11

ISLAM

Be they men or women, those that embrace the Faith
   and do what is right, We will surely grant a happy life;
We shall reward them according to their noblest deeds.

Qur'an 16.97

Allah has promised to believers . . .
    beautiful mansions in Gardens of everlasting bliss.
But the greatest bliss is the good pleasure of Allah:
    that is the grand achievement.

Qur'an 9.72

BUDDHISM

All those who are unhappy in the world are so
    as a result of their desire for their own happiness.
All those who are happy in the world are so
    as a result of their desire for the happiness of others.

A Guide to the Bodhisattva Way of Life 8.129

HINDUISM

If one is able to tolerate the urges of the material senses
    and check the force of desire and anger,
such a one is well situated and is happy in this world.

Bhagavad Gita 5.23

The Infinite is the source of joy.
    There is no joy in the finite.
Only in the Infinite is there joy.
    Ask to know the Infinite.

Chandogya Upanishad 7.23

JUDAISM

There is deceit in the hearts of those who plot evil,
    but joy for those who promote peace.

Proverbs 12.20*

You show me the path of life.
In your presence there is fullness of joy;
    in your right hand are pleasures forevermore.

Psalm 16.11*

CONFUCIANISM

The noble-minded delight in three things . . .
That family members are alive and well—this is one delight.
That they have no reason to feel shame before Heaven,
    and they have no reason to blush before people—
    this is a second delight.
That they can teach and nourish excellent students—
    this is the third delight.

Mencius VII.A.20

TAOISM

If you want to expand the field of happiness,
lay the foundation of it on the bottom of your heart
    where good deeds originate.

Tract of the Quiet Way

don't be greedy.

WHEN THERE IS GREED, THE LOVE IS FALSE.

SIKHISM. *Guru Granth Sahib, Shalok, Farid, p. 1378*

CHRISTIANITY

Take care! Be on your guard against all kinds of greed;
for one's life does not consist
    in the abundance of possessions.

Luke 12.15

The love of money is a root of all kinds of evil.

1 Timothy 6.10

ISLAM

Those who preserve themselves from their own greed
    will surely prosper.

Qur'an 59.9

BUDDHISM

The greedy will not find their way to the heaven realms.
It is the fool who does not see the good in giving.

Dhammapada 177

Creatures are scorched by the fire of greed,
   which feeds on sense-objects as its fuel.

Ashvaghosha, Buddhacarita

HINDUISM

O my wealth-coveting and foolish soul,
when will you succeed in emancipating yourself
   from the desire for wealth?
Shame on my foolishness! I have been your toy!
It is thus that one becomes a slave of others.
No one born on earth did ever attain to the end of desire . . .
   The desire for wealth can never bring happiness.

Mahabharata, Santiparva 177.25-26

JUDAISM

Better one handful with tranquility
   than two handfuls with toil and chasing after the wind.

Ecclesiastes 4.6*

Give me neither poverty nor riches,
   but give me only my daily bread.
Otherwise, I may have too much and disown you and say,
   "Who is the Lord?"
Or I may become poor and steal,
   and so dishonor the name of my God.

Proverbs 30.8-9*

CONFUCIANISM

The chase of gain is rich in hate.

Analects 4.12

The greatest curse is discontent.
The greatest calamity is greed.

Tao Te Ching 46

Evildoers are greedy and covetous without satiety.

Treatise on Response & Retribution, part 3

give up transient riches to gain everlasting treasure.

O SHREWD BUSINESSPERSON, DO ONLY PROFITABLE BUSINESS:

DEAL ONLY IN THAT COMMODITY

THAT WILL ACCOMPANY YOU AFTER DEATH.

SIKHISM. *Guru Granth Sahib, Sri Raga, p. 22*

CHRISTIANITY

Do not store up for yourselves treasures on earth,
    where moth and rust destroy
    and where thieves break in and steal,
but store up for yourselves treasures in heaven . . .
For where your treasure is, there your heart will be also.

Matthew 6.19-21

What good will it be for you if you gain the whole world,
    yet forfeit your soul?

Matthew 16.26

ISLAM

Your worldly riches are transitory,
    but Allah's reward is everlasting.

Qur'an 16.95

[221]

Are the ones who lay their foundation on duty
      to Allah and his good pleasure better,
or the ones who lay their foundation
      on the edge of a cracking hollowed bank,
so it breaks down with them into the fire of hell?

Qur'an 9.109

BUDDHISM

You who wish for happiness without the sting of regret,
      lead a life of righteousness.
You who yearn for riches, receive treasures that are eternal.
Truth is wealth, and a life of truth is happiness.

Gospel of Buddha 2.8

Let those who are wise do righteousness:
A treasure . . . which no thief can steal;
      a treasure which does not pass away.

Khuddakapatha 8.9

HINDUISM

I know that treasures pass away
      and that the Eternal is not reached by the transient.

Katha Upanishad 1.2.10

To him I will come when I go beyond this life.
And to him will come the one who has faith
      and doubts not . . .
I go to the Imperishable Treasure: by his grace,
      by his grace, by his grace.

Chandogya Upanishad 3.14.4; 3.15.3

Wisdom is more profitable than silver
    and yields better returns than gold.
She is more precious than rubies;
    nothing you desire can compare with her.

*Proverbs 3.14-15**

Turn my eyes away from worthless things . . .
The law from your mouth is more precious to me
    than thousands of pieces of silver and gold.

*Psalm 119.37, 72**

CONFUCIANISM

If you cultivate wealth, you give up Humanity.
    If you cultivate Humanity, you give up wealth.

Mencius III.A.3

TAOISM

The wise wear common clothes
    and carry jewels in their hearts.

Tao Te Ching 70

detach from the temporal;
attach to the eternal.

BUSY NOT YOURSELF WITH THIS WORLD,

FOR WITH FIRE WE TEST THE GOLD,

AND WITH GOLD WE TEST OUR SERVANTS.

BAHA'I FAITH. *Hidden Words of Bahá'u'lláh, Part I*

(From the Arabic) 55

CHRISTIANITY

Do not love the world or the things in the world . . .
The world and its desires pass away,
    but whoever does the will of God lives forever.

I John 2.15, 17

We fix our eyes not on what is seen, but on what is unseen.
For what is seen is temporary,
    but what is unseen is eternal . . .
We live by faith, not by sight.

II Corinthians 4.18; 5.7

ISLAM

Allah has purchased from the faithful their lives
    and worldly goods
and in return has promised them the Garden . . .
Rejoice then in the bargain you have made.
    That is the supreme triumph.

Qur'an 9.111

BUDDHISM

Empty the boat and it will sail smoothly for you.
Throw overboard all desire and hate,
    and you will reach nirvana.

Dhammapada 369

It is not that I despise the objects of sense,
and I know full well that they make up
    what we call the "world."
But when I consider the impermanence
    of everything in this world,
then I can find no delight in it.

Ashvaghosha, Buddhacarita

HINDUISM

The mature person, fulfilled in wisdom, resolute,
    looks with equal detachment at a lump of dirt,
    a rock, or a piece of pure gold.

Bhagavad Gita 6.8

Let attachment to the Lord be your one attachment.
That attachment will help you to free yourself
    from other attachments.

Tirukkural 350

Though your riches increase,
    do not set your heart on them.

*Psalm 62.10**

One does not live on bread alone
but on every word that comes from the mouth of the Lord.

*Deuteronomy 8.3**

CONFUCIANISM

I love life, but I also love righteousness.
    If I must make a choice, I will choose righteousness.

Mencius VI.A.10

TAOISM

Shape clay into a vessel;
    it is the space within that makes it useful.
Cut doors and windows for a room;
    it is the holes which make it useful.
Therefore profit comes from what is there;
    usefulness from what is not there.

Tao Te Ching 11

breathing

just about every major religion agrees that "breathing" carries a deeper meaning than simple respiration. Taoism portrays breathing as a means of purification. When we exhale, we get rid of the worn out and old; when we inhale, we receive the new and fresh.

Christians Muslims and Jews equate breath with life itself. After all, Adam became a living soul only after "God breathed into him the breath of life." In the Christian New Testament, the "Holy Spirit" can literally be translated as the "Holy Breath."

Doctors worldwide now recognize that breathing exercises elicit a "relaxation response." Studies show that this mind-body calming technique reduces hypertension, headaches, insomnia, anxiety, poor digestion, and other ills.

Buddhists say that Anapana-sati, a breathing awareness meditation, is the gateway to enlightenment, a way to cultivate Right Mindfulness. This mindfulness enables us to discard controlling thoughts of "I" and "mine."

BREATHING AWARENESS MEDITATION

1. Find a quiet place and sit in the Lotus pose (shown to the right). If this is uncomfortable, you can sit in a half-cross-legged position—

with one leg straight, and one leg bent. Hold your body erect but not rigid, keeping your spine straight.

2. Close your eyes.

3. Fix your attention on the place where your breaths enter and leave the nostrils. Keep your attention on that spot, as a sentry watching a gate. Brush away any thoughts or sensations but those of breathing in and out.

4. Continue this for about ten minutes. Don't control your breathing. Don't try to breathe deeply or hold your breath. Breathe comfortably, and simply watch the breathing. This exercise is one of observing reality as it is, without any preferences or reactions.

Hindus tell us there is a direct relationship between how we breathe and how we think. Thoughts of fear, loneliness, despair, and frustration can disappear through a practice called "Rhythmic Breathing." In this exercise, we can tune into the rhythm of the Universe and surrender our thoughts of separateness and striving:

RHYTHMIC BREATHING

1. Sit in a comfortable cross-legged position, or on a chair with your legs uncrossed. Loosen any tight clothing. Make sure your spine is straight.

2. Take a few deep, slow breaths, allowing your abdomen to expand fully each time you inhale. Deeply relax your muscles, starting from your feet and working your way up your body.

3. Find the pulse in your wrist. Listen carefully and count 1-2-3-4 several times, until you fall into this rhythm and can follow it without holding your pulse. Continue mentally counting 1-2-3-4, and place your hands on your knees.

4. Take a deep breath while counting 1-2-3-4; hold the breath for a count of two; then exhale while counting 1-2-3-4.

5. Repeat as long as 20 minutes, or as little as a few seconds. Try it when you feel anxious or frustrated. Try it whenever you need to "let go."

bibliography

Abimbola, Wande, ed. *Yoruba Oral Tradition*. Ibadan, Nigeria: University Press, 1975.

Access Foundation. (2002). *The Quran: Standard English Version*. Edited by Renee Lloyd. Translated by Zaine Ridling. http://www.anova.org/sev/htm/qr (Accessed 29 Apr 2003).

African Proverbs, Stories and Sayings. (1999-2003). "Daily African Proverbs from Missionary Service News Agency and Other Sources." Nairobi. 28 Apr 2000, 26 Apr 2001, 27 Apr 2001, 19 Jun 2001, 30 Jul 2002. http://www.afriprov.org/resources/dailyproverbs.htm (Accessed 29 Apr 2003).

Ahmad, Ghazi, trans. *Sayings of Muhammad*. Lahore, Pakistan: Sh. Muhammad Ashraf, 1968.

Ali, Abdullah Yusuf, trans. *The Holy Qur'an: Text, Translation & Commentary*. Lahore: Sh. Muhammad Ashraf, 1938.

Ali, Abdullah Yusuf, trans. *The Meaning of the Holy Qur'an*, 10th ed. Reprint, Beltsville, MD: Amana Publications, 2003.

Ali, Maulana Muhammad, trans. *A Manual of Hadith*. Columbus: Ahmadiyya Anjuman Ishaat Islam Lahore, 2001.

Ali, Maulana Muhammad, trans. *The Holy Qur'an: Arabic Text with English Translation, Commentary, and Comprehensive Introduction*. Columbus: Ahmadiyya Anjuman Ishaat Islam Lahore, 2002.

[231]

Arnold, Sir Edwin, trans. *Bhagavadgita*. 1885. Reprint, New York: Dover Publications, 1993.

Aston, W. G. "Oracle of Temmangu," in *Shinto: The Way of the Gods*. London: Longmans, Green & Co., 1905.

Bahá'u'lláh. *Gleanings, from the Writings of Bahá'u'lláh*. Translated by Shogi Effendi. Wilmette, IL: Baha'i Publishing Trust, 1951.

Bahá'u'lláh. *The Hidden Words of Bahá'u'lláh*. Wilmette, IL: Baha'i Publishing Committee, 1954.

Baron, Joseph L., ed. *A Treasury of Jewish Quotations*. Northvale, NJ: Jason Aronson, 1985.

Basu, B. D., ed. *The Matsya Puranam*. Sacred Books of the Hindus, vol. 17. Translated by A. Taluqdar of Oudh. 1917. Reprint, New York: AMS Press, 1974.

Batchelor, Stephen, trans. *A Guide to the Bodhisattva's Way of Life: The Bodhisattvacharyavatara by Acharya Shantideva*. Dharamsala, India: Library of Tibetan Works and Archives, 1979.

Baynes, Cary F., trans. *The I Ching: or, Book of Changes. The Richard Wilhelm Translation Rendered into English by Cary F. Baynes*. Princeton: Princeton University Press, 1967.

Beck, Sanderson, comp. *The Wisdom Bible*. Ojai, CA: World Peace Communications, 2002.

Berkson, William Koller. (1999). *The Book of Principles: The Ethical Classic Pirkei Avot*. Tel Aviv University and The Shalom Hartman Institute for Advanced Jewish Studies. http://mentsh.com/pirkei_avot.html (Accessed 30 Mar 2003).

Bhikkhu, Thanissaro, trans. *Dhammapada*. Barre, MA: Dhamma Dana Publications, 1997.

Blakney, Raymond B., trans. *The Way of Life: A New Translation (Tao Te Ching)*. New York: Penguin, New American Library, 1955.

Bloomfield, Maurice, trans. *Hymns of the Atharva-Veda: Together with Extracts from the Ritual Books and the Commentaries*. Sacred Books of the East, vol. 42. edited by Friedrich Max Muller, 1897. Reprint, Delhi: Motilal Banarsidass, 1964.

Bose, Abinash Chandra. *The Call of the Vedas*. Bombay: Bharatiya Vidya Bhavan, 1954.

Bose, Abinash Chandra, ed. *Hymns from the Vedas*. Bombay: Asia Publishing House, 1966.

Brar, Sandeep Singh. (1998). "Sri Guru Granth Sahib in English Translation. Translated by Dr. Sant Singh Khalsa." *The Sikhism Home Page.* http://www.sikhs.org/english/egranth.htm. [Accessed 29 Apr 2003].

Buddharakkhita, Acharya, trans. *The Dhammapada: The Buddha's Path of Wisdom.* Kandy, Sri Lanka: Buddhist Publication Society, 1985.

Bühler, Georg, trans. *The Laws of Manu.* Sacred Books of the East, vol. 25, edited by Friedrich Max Muller, 1886. Reprint, New York: Dover Publications, 1969.

Bukhari, Muhammad Ibn Ismail. *The English Translation of Hadith of Al Bukhari with the Arabic Text,* 9 vols. Translated by Muhammad Muhsin Khan. Lahore, Pakistan: Kazi Publications, 1993.

Bunzel, Ruth. "Zuni Ritual Poetry," *The Forty-Seventh Annual Report of the Bureau of American Ethnology.* Washington, D. C.: The Smithsonian Institution, 1929-30.

Burnell, Arthur Coke, ed. *The Ordinances of Manu.* London: Trubner, 1884.

Byrom, Thomas, trans. *Dhammapada: The Sayings of the Buddha.* Boulder, CO: Shambhala Publications, 1993.

Carus, Paul, comp. *Gospel of Buddha.* 1894. Reprint, Chicago: Open Court Publishing, 1991.

Champion, Selwyn Gurney and Dorothy Short, comp. "Oracle of the Kami of Itsukushima," in *Readings from World Religions.* Greenwich, CT: Fawcett Publications, 1963.

Chang, Garma C. C., ed. *A Treasury of Mahayana Sutras: Selections from the Maharatnakuta Sutra.* University Park and London: Pennsylvania State University Press, 1983.

Cheung, William, ed. *The Lun Yu in English.* Hong Kong: Confucius Publishing Co., 1996.

Cleary, Thomas F., trans. *The Flower Ornament Scripture: A Translation of the Avatamsaka Sutra,* vol. I. Boulder, CO: Shambhala Publications, 1984.

Cohen, Abraham, ed. *Everyman's Talmud.* London: J. M. Dent; New York: E. P. Dutton, 1949.

Conze, Edward, trans. "Asita's Visit." and "Withdrawal from Women." (excerpts from *Ashvagosha, Buddhacarita*) Pt. I, ch. 2 of *Buddhist Scriptures.* New York: Penguin Classics, 1959.

Danby, Herbert, trans. *The Mishnah*. London: Oxford University Press, 1933.

Dawood, N. J., trans. *The Koran*. Fifth revised ed. London: Penguin Classics, 1990.

Dawud, Abu. *Sunan Abu Dawud: English translation*, 3 vols. Translated by Ahmad Hasan. New Delhi: Kitab Bhavan, 2000.

Deguchi, Onisaburo. *A Guide to God's Way*. Translated by R. J. Hammer. Kameoka, Japan: Omoto Kyo, 1957.

de Ley, Gerd, ed. *African Proverbs*. New York, Hippocrene Books, 1999.

Dermenghem, Emile. *Muhammad and the Islamic Tradition*. Translated by Jean M. Watt. New York: Harper, 1958. Reprint, Woodstock, NY: Overlook Press, 1981.

Dharma Publishing Staff, trans. *Dhammapada*. Berkeley, CA: Dharma Publishing, 1985.

Dutt, Manmatha Natha, ed. *The Garuda Purana*. Calcutta: Society for the Resuscitation of Indian Literature, 1908.

Edmunds, Albert J. *Buddhist and Christian Gospels*, 4th ed., 2 vols. edited by Masaharu Anesaki. Philadelphia: Innes and Sons, 1914.

Eddy, Mary Baker. *Science and Health, with Key to the Scriptures*. 1910. Reprint, Captiva, FL: Mary Baker Eddy Foundation, 1986.

Eknath Easwaran, ed. and trans. *The Bhagavad Gita*. Tomales, CA: Nilgiri Press, 1985.

Eliot, Charles W., ed. "The Sayings of Confucius," in *The Harvard Classics*, vol. XLIV. New York: P. F. Collier & Son, 1909-10.

Ellis, Alfred Burdon. *Yoruba-Speaking Peoples of the Slave Coast of West Africa: Their Religion, Manners, Customs, Laws and Language*. 1894. Reprint, Oosterhout N. B., Netherlands: Anthropological Publications, 1966.

Epstein, Isidore, ed. *The Babylonian Talmud*. New York: Soncino Press, 1948.

Freedman, Harry and Maurice Simon, trans. *Midrash Rabbah*. New York: Soncino Press, 1983.

Freke, Timothy. *The Illustrated Book of Sacred Scriptures*. Wheaton, IL: Theosophical Publishing House; Quest Books; Alresford, UK: Godsfield Press, 1998.

Ganguli, Kisarai Mohan, trans. *The Mahabharata of Krishna-Dwaipayana Vyasa*. New Delhi: Munshiram Manoharlal, 1982.

Ganson, C., trans. *Tao Te Ching*. Daoism Depot.http://www.edepot. com/tao13.html (Accessed 6 Jul 2003).

Goddard, Dwight. "Surangama Sutra," in *A Buddhist Bible*. Boston: Beacon Press, 1994.

Goldin, Judah, trans. *The Living Talmud: The Wisdom of the Fathers*. New York: Penguin, New American Library, 1957.

Havens, Norman. *The World of Shinto*. Tokyo: Bukkyo Dendo Kyokai, 1985.

Herford, R. Travers, ed. *The Ethics of the Talmud: Sayings of the Fathers*. New York: Schocken Books, 1962.

Hinton, David, trans. *The Analects: Confucius*. Washington, D.C.: Perseus Books Group, Counterpoint, 1998.

Hinton, David, trans. *Mencius*. Washington, D. C.: Perseus Books Group, Counterpoint, 1999.

The Holy Bible, New International Version. Grand Rapids, MI: Zondervan Publishing House, 1985.

The Holy Bible, New Revised Standard Version. London: Collins Publishers, Division of Christian Education of the National Council of the Churches in the United States of America, 1989.

Hurvitz, Leon, trans. *Scripture of the Lotus Blossom of the Fine Dharma*. New York: Columbia University Press, 1976.

Ireland, John D. Ireland, trans. "The Discourse Collection: Selected Texts from the Sutta Nipata." *"Wheel" Publication No. 82*. Kandy, Sri Lanka: Buddhist Publication Society, 1983.

Jacobi, Hermann, trans. *The Jaina Sutras*, vol. 1. Sacred Books of the East, vol. 22, edited by Friedrich Max Muller. 1884. Reprint, New York: Dover Publications, 1968.

Jain, S. A., trans. *Reality: English translation of Shri Pujyapada's Sarvarthasiddhi*. Calcutta: Vira Sasana Sangha, 1960.

Judge, William Quan, trans. (1890). *Bhagavad Gita*. Theosophical University Press Online Edition.http://www.theosociety.org/ pasadena/gita/bg-eg-hp.htm (Accessed 7 Jul 2003).

Kato, Genchi. *Shinto in Essence*. Tokyo: Nogi Shrine, 1954.

Kaviratna, Harischandra, ed. and trans. *Dhammapada: Wisdom of the Buddha*. Pasadena: Theosophical University Press, 1980.

Khalifa, Rhashad, trans. *Qur'an: The Final Testament*. Fremont, CA: Universal Unity, 2001.

Khoroche, Peter, trans. *Once the Buddha Was a Monkey: Arya Sura's Jatakamala*. Chicago: University of Chicago, 1989.

Kundakunda. *Pancastikaya of Kundakunda*. Translated by Anand Chakravarti. New Delhi: Bharatiya Jnanapeeth, 1944.

Lau, D. C., trans. *Mencius*. London: Penguin Classics, 1970.

Lau, D. C., trans. *Tao Te Ching*. London: Penguin Classics, 1963.

Legge, James, trans. *The Chinese Classics: With a Translation, Critical and Exegetical Notes, Prolegomena, and Copious Indexes*, 5 vols. Oxford: Clarendon Press, 1893-1895.

Legge, James, trans. *The Li Chi: Book of Rites*, vol. 2. Sacred Books of the East, vol. 28. edited by Friedrich Max Muller, 1885. Reprint, Kila, MT: Kessinger Publishing, 2003.

Legge, James, trans. "The Writings of Chuang Tzu" and "Book of Ritual" in *The Sacred Books of China: The Texts of Taoism*, vol. 2. Sacred Books of the East, vol. 27. edited by Friedrich Max Muller, 1879-85. Reprint, New York: Dover Publications, 1962.

Leslau, Charlotte and Wolf Leslau, comp. *African Proverbs*. Mount Vernon, NY: Peter Pauper Press, 1962.

Marpa Foundation. [21 Aug 1997]. *Aspiration Prayer of Maitreya, Ratnakuta Sutra*. Translated by Michele Martin with the assistance of Karl Brunnholzl and Chryssoula Zerbini under the guidance of Khenpo Tsultrim Gyamtso Rinpoche. http://www.namoguru.org/teach ings.html (Accessed 29 Apr 2003).

Mascaro, Juan, trans. *Dhammapada*. London: Penguin, 1973.

Mascaro, Juan, trans. *The Upanishads*. London: Penguin Classics, 1965.

McCarroll, Tolbert, trans. *The Tao: The Sacred Way*. New York: Crossroad Publishing, 1982.

McDonald, John H., trans. (1996-2003). *Tao Te Ching*. http://www.geocities.com/shoshindojo/index.html (Accessed 6 Jul 2003).

McNaughton, William. *The Confucian Vision*. Ann Arbor: University of Michigan Press, 1974.

Merel, Peter A., ed. (1995). *Tao Te Ching: An English Language Interpolation based on the translations of Robert G. Henricks, Lin Yutang, D.C. Lau, Ch'u Ta-Kao, Gia-Fu Feng & Jane English, Richard Wilhelm and Aleister Crowley*. http://www.chinapage.org/gnl.html (Accessed 29 Apr 2003).

Merton, Thomas, ed. and trans. *The Way of Chuang Tzu*. New York: New Directions Publishing, 1965.

Mitchell, Stephen, trans. *Bhagavad Gita: A New Translation*. New York: Random House, Three Rivers Press, 2002.

Mitchell, Stephen. *Tao Te Ching by Lao Tzu: A New English Version with Foreward and Notes*. New York: HarperCollins Publishers, 1988.

Moon, Sun Myung. *Moon Sun Myung Sensaeng Malseum Seonjip* (Selections from Rev. Sun Myung Moon's Words), over 100 vols. Translated by the Institute for the Rev. Sun Myung Moon's Sermons and Speeches at Sung Hwa University. Seoul, Korea: Holy Spirit Association for the Unification of World Christianity, 1984.

Moses, Jeffrey. *Oneness: Great Principles Shared by All Religions*. New York: Random House, Ballantine Publishing, 2002.

Muller, Charles A., trans. (01 Apr 2003). "Five Chinese Classics." *Resources for East Asian Language and Thought*.http://www.human.toyogakuen-u.ac.jp/~acmuller/fiveclassics.htm (Accessed 29 Apr 2003).

Muller, Friedrich Max, ed. and trans. *The Dhammapada*. Sacred Books of the East, vol. X. Oxford: Clarendon Press, 1881.

Muller, Friedrich Max, ed. and trans. *Upanishads,* part II. Sacred Books of the East, vol. 15. 1884. Reprint, New York: Dover Publications, 1962.

Nakayama, Miki. *Ofudesaki: The Tip of the Writing Brush*. Tenri City, Japan: The Headquarters of Tenrikyo Church, 1971.

Nanamoli, Bhikkhu and Bhikkhu Bodhi, trans. *The Middle Length Discourses of the Buddha: A New Translation of the Majjhima Nikaya. Original translation by Bhikkhu Ñanamoli; translation edited and revised by Bhikkhu Bodhi*. Kandy, Sri Lanka: Buddhist Publication Society, 1995.

An-Nawawi, Yahia bin Sharaful-Deen, comp. *An-Nawawi's Forty Hadiths*. Translated by Denys Johnson-Davies and Ezzeddin Ibrahim. Cambridge, UK: Islamic Texts Society, 1997.

Nerburn, Kent and Louise Menglekoch. *Native American Wisdom*. Classic Wisdom Collection. San Rafael, CA: New World Library, 1991.

Neusner, Jacob and Noam M. M. Neusner, eds. *The Book of Jewish Wisdom*. New York: Continuum Publishing, 1996.

Newman, Louis I. and Samuel Spitz, eds. *The Talmudic Anthology*. New York: Behrman House, 1945.

Norman, K. R., trans. *The Group of Discourses*. London: Pali Text Society, 1984.

Norman, K. R., trans. "Sutta Nipata," in *The Rhinoceros Horn: and Other Early Buddhist Poems*. London: Pali Text Society, 1984.

Numata, Yehan. *The Teaching of Buddha*. Tokyo: Bukkyo Dendo Kyokai, 1977.

Nurbakhsh, Javad, comp. *Traditions of the Prophet*. Translated by Kabir Helminski. New York: Khaniqahi-Nimatullahi Publications, 1981.

O'Flaherty, Wendy Doniger, trans. *The Rig Veda*. London: Penguin Books, 1981.

Ollivier, John J. *The Wisdom of African Mythology*. Largo, FL: Top of the Mountain Publishing, 1994.

Ottley, Warren S., Sr. "Nga Whakatauki: Proverbial Maori Sayings" *Warren's World*. http://www.burgoyne.com/pages/wso (Accessed 29 Apr 2003).

Pachocinski, Ryszard. *Proverbs of Africa: Human Nature in the Nigerian Oral Tradition*. St. Paul: Professors World Peace Academy, 1996.

Panikkar, Raimundo, trans. *The Vedic Experience: Mantramanjari (an Anthology of the Vedas for Modern Man and Contemporary Celebration)*. Columbia, MO: South Asia Books, 2001.

Pickthall, Mohammed Marmaduke, trans. *Holy Qur'an*. Delhi: Kutub Khana Ishaat-ul-Islam, 1970.

Prabhavananda, Swami and Christopher Isherwood, trans. *The Song of God: Bhagavad-Gita*. New York: Penguin, New American Library, 1972.

Prabhavananda, Swami, trans. *The Spiritual Heritage of India*. Garden City, NY: Doubleday, 1963.

Prabhavananda, Swami, ed. and trans. *Srimad Bhagavatam: The Wisdom of God*. Mylapore, Madras: Sri Ramakrishna Math, 1947.

Prabhupada, A. C. Bhaktivedanta Swami. *Bhagavad-gita As It Is*. Los Angeles: Bhaktivedanta Book Trust, 1984.

Prasad, Ramanand, trans. (1988) *Bhagavad Gita.* Fremont, CA: American Gita Society. http://eawc.evansville.edu/anthology/gita.htm (Accessed 7 Jul 2003).

Radhakrishnan, Sarvepalli and Charles A. Moore, ed. *A Source Book in Indian Philosophy.* Princeton, NJ: Princeton University Press, 1957.

Richards, John, trans. (1993) "Dhammapada." *Books-on-Line.com.* http://www.books-online.com/bol/BookDisplay.cfm?BookNum=1125 (Accessed 29 Apr 2003).

Rosenfeld, Rabbi Dovid and Project Genesis, Inc. "Chapters of Our Fathers." *Pirkei-Avos.* http://www.torah.org/learning/pirkeiavos/ (Accessed 29 Apr 2003).

Rosenthal, Stanley (Shi-tien Roshi), trans. (1984) *Tao Te Ching.* Cardiff, Wales, UK: British School of Zen Taoism. http://departments.col gate.edu/greatreligions/pages/buddhanet/zen325/zentao/TAOTE4-5.TXT (Accessed 6 Jul 2003).

Ryerson University. *Tri-Mentoring Monthly.* Winter semester, Jan. 2002. http://www.ryerson.ca/trimentoring/Newsletters/Tri-News-Jan02.pdf (Accessed 29 Apr 2003).

Saddhatissa, Hammalawa, trans. *The Sutta-Nipata.* London: Curzon Press, 1985.

Saldarini, Anthony J., trans. *The Fathers According to Rabbi Nathan.* Leiden, Netherlands: E. J. Brill, 1975.

Shantideva. *A Guide to the Bodhisattva Way of Life: Bodhicaryavatara.* Translated by Vesna A. Wallace and B. Alan Wallace. Ithaca, NY: Snow Lion Publications, 1997.

Siddiqui, Abdul Hameed, trans. *Sahih Muslim.* Chicago: Kazi Publications, 1976.

Singh, Harbans, trans. *The Message of Sikhism.* Delhi: Delhi Sikhi Gurdwara Management Committee, 1978.

Sparham, Gareth, trans. *The Tibetan Dhammapada: Sayings of the Buddha—A Translation of the Tibetan Version of the Udanavarga.* London: Wisdom Publications, 1986.

Suzuki, Daisetz Teitaro and Paul Carus, trans. *Yin Chih Wen: Tract of the Quiet Way, with Extracts from the Chinese Commentary.* Chicago, Open Court Publishing, 1906.

Talib, Hazrat Ali Ibn Abi. *Nahjul Balagha of Hazrat Ali*. Translated by Syed Mohammed Askari Jafery. Pathergatti, India: Seerat-Uz-Zahra Committee, 1965.

Talib, Hazrat Ali Ibn Abi. *Nahjul Balagha: Peak of Eloquence: Sermons and Letters of Imam Ali Ibn Abi Talib*. Translated by Sayed Ali Reza. Bombay: Imam Foundation, 1989.

Talib, Gurbachan Singh, trans. *Sri Guru Granth Sahib*, 4 vols. Patiala: Publication Bureau of Punjabi University, 1984.

Taylor, John V. *The Primal Vision*, 4th ed. London: SCM Press, 1975.

Telang, Kashinath Trimbak Telang, trans. *Bhagavad Gita: with the Sanatsugatiya and the Anugita*. Sacred Books of the East, vol. 8. edited by Friedrich Max Muller, 1882. Reprint, Oxford: Clarendon Press, 1908.

Thera, Narada Maha, ed. and trans. *Dhammapada: Sayings of Buddha (Wisdom of the East Series)*. London: John Murray (Publishers) Ltd., 1954.

Thera, Nyanaponika and Bhikku Bodhi, ed. and trans. *Numerical Discourses of the Buddha: An Anthology of Suttas from the Anguttara Nikaya*. Kandy, Sri Lanka: Buddhist Publication Society, 1999.

Tiruvalluvar. *Weaver's Wisdom: Ancient Precepts for a Perfect Life*. Translated by Satguru Sivaya Subramuniyaswami. Kapaa, HI: Himalayan Academy Publications, 1999.

Tiruvalluvar. *Kural: The Great Book of Tiru-Valluvar*. Translated by Shri C. Rajagopalachari (Rajaji). Mumbai, India: Bharatiya Vidya Bhavan, 1996.

Tiruvalluvar. *Tiruvalluvar: The Kural*. Translated by P. S. Sundaram. London: Penguin Books, 1990.

Tsu, Lao. *Tao Te Ching*. Translated by Gia-fu Feng and Jane English. New York: Random House, Alfred A. Knopf, 1997.

Tze, Lao. *Treatise on Response & Retribution*. Translated by Daisetz Teitaro Suzuki and Paul Carus. LaSalle, IL: Open Court Publishing, 1973.

Tzu, Lao. *Tao Te Ching: The Wisdom of Laotse*. Edited and translated by Lin Yutang. New York: Random House, Modern Library, 1948.

Waley, Arthur, trans. *The Analects of Confucius*. London: George Allen & Unwin, 1938.

Walker, Brian, trans. *Hua Hu Ching: The Unknown Teachings of Lao Tzu.* New York: HarperSan Francisco, 1992.

Wannapok, Santhienpong, trans. *Dhammapada: A Collection of Verses Containing the Buddha's Essential Teachings.* Buddhism Depot. http://www.edepot.com/dhamma4.html (Accessed 10 Jul 2003).

Watson, Burton, ed. and trans. *Complete Works of Chuang Tzu.* New York: Columbia University Press, 1968.

Watson, Burton, trans. *The Lotus Sutra.* New York: Columbia University Press, 1993.

Welker, Glenn, comp. (1996-2003). "Chief Tecumseh: Shawnee." *Indigenous Peoples Literature.* http://www.indigenouspeople.net /tecumseh.htm (Accessed 29 Apr 2003).

West, Edward William, trans. *Zend-Avesta.* Sacred Books of the East, vol. 24, edited by Friedrich Max Muller, 1885. Reprint, Delhi: Motilal Banarsidass, 1965.

Wilson, Andrew, ed. *World Scripture.* New York: Paragon House Publishers, 1991.

Wilson, Horace H., trans. *The Vishnu Purana: A System of Hindu Mythology and Tradition.* London: Printed for the Oriental Translation Fund of Great Britain and Ireland, 1840.

Witness-Pioneer, An Islamic Webgroup. (16 Sep 2002). "Khalifa Umar bin al-Khattab: The Farewell Pilgrimage." *A Virtual Library of Witness-Pioneer.* http://www.witness-pioneer.org/vil/Articles/ companion/10_umar_bin_ al_ khattab .htm (Accessed 29 Apr 2003).

Woodward, Frank Lee and Edward M. Hare, trans. *The Book of Gradual Sayings (Anguttara Nikaya),* 5 vols. Translation Series, nos. 22, 24-27. London: Pali Text Society, 1994.

Woodward, Frank Lee, trans. *Minor Anthologies of the Pali Canon: Part 2, Udana: Verses of Uplift and Itivuttaka: As It Was Said.* London: Pali Text Society, 1948.

Woodward, Frank Lee., trans. *Some Sayings of the Buddha.* London: Oxford University Press, 1973.

Xun, Zhou, with T. H. Barrett, comp. *The Wisdom of the Confucians.* Oxford, UK: Oneworld Publications, 2001.

Yamamoto, Kosho. *Mahaparinirvana Sutra*, 3 vols. Ube City: Karinbunko, 1973-75.

Yuen, Ko (Aleister Crowley), trans. *The Tao Teh King: Liber CLVII*. 1918. Reprint, London: Askin Publishers, 1976.

Yun, Hsing. "Six Things to be Mindful of," in *Epoch of the Buddha's Light*. Translated by Yi Jih and Tom Graham (BLIA International Translation Center). Taipei: Buddha's Light International Association: Fo Guang Publishing, 1997.

Yutang, Lin, ed. and trans. *The Wisdom of China and India*. New York: Random House, Modern Library, 1955.

Yutang, Lin, ed. and trans. *The Wisdom of Confucius*. New York: Random House, Modern Library, 1994.

Zona, Guy A., comp. *The Soul Would Have No Rainbow if the Eyes Had No Tears: and Other Native American Proverbs*. New York: Simon & Schuster, 1994.

permissions

CPSIA information can be obtained at www.ICGtesting.com
Printed in the USA
LVOW07s0324150216

475053LV00044B/79/P